» Simple Guides
JUDAISM

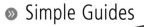

» Simple Guides

JUDAISM

David Starr-Glass

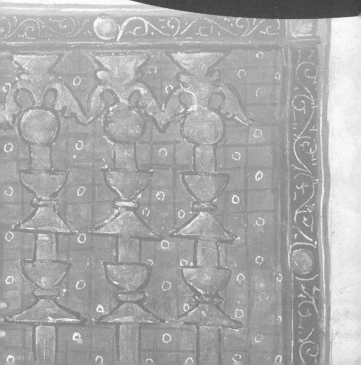

Published in Great Britain by
Simple Guides, an imprint of Bravo Ltd
59 Hutton Grove, London N12 8DS
www.kuperard.co.uk
Enquiries: office@kuperard.co.uk

First published 1997 by Global Books Ltd.
This edition published 2008

ISBN 978 1 85733 440 1

British Library Cataloguing in Publication Data
A CIP catalogue entry for this book
is available from the British Library

Printed in Malaysia

About the Author

DAVID STARR-GLASS is a senior lecturer in management studies at several American campuses in Jerusalem. Born and educated in Scotland, he worked extensively in California before emigrating to Israel in 1983. His writings include an autobiography (*Gathered Stones*. Feldheim: 1994) and cross-cultural studies, including *A Simple Guide to Customs and Etiquette in Israel* (Global Books: 1996).

⊙ Contents

List of Illustrations

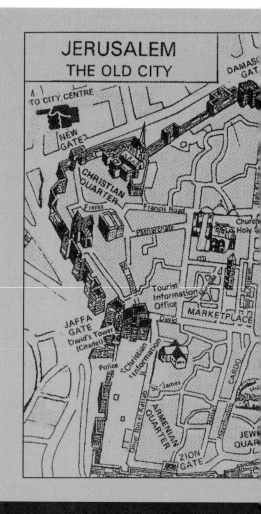

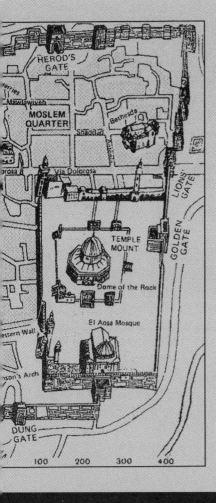

HEROD'S
GATE

Mawlawiyeh

MOSLEM
QUARTER

Shaddad

Bethesda

Via Dolorosa

orosa

Via Dolorosa

LION'S
GATE

GOLDEN GATE

TEMPLE
MOUNT

Dome of the Rock

El Aqsa Mosque

Western Wall

son's Arch

DUNG
GATE

100   200   300   400

The Torah begins with the second letter of the alphabet, and each tractate of the Talmud begins with page two, to suggest that the human mind cannot comprehend the perfect unity [the 'alef'; the 'one'] which preceded God's revelation of His being.

RABBINICAL SAYING

There was a time when if we wanted to know something about another culture we went to a museum. We would look at objects – masks, pots, baskets, weapons, ritual articles, clothes – and tried to imagine who had made these things and why. And, of course, we remained essentially isolated and unconnected to the vibrancy which had created these artifacts. Today, we recognize that to appreciate a culture other than our own is to make a conscious voyage of discovery: it is to attempt to understand the patterns which shape the lives and actions of those who are not us; an attempt to remain open to newness and to take intellectual risks.

Many consider that in trying to appreciate another culture it is helpful if someone within the culture attempts to guide those on its outside.

⊙ *A scribe writing on the parchment scroll of a* Sefer Torah

Rather than look at display cases of glass, the person exploring the new culture is encouraged to walk beyond the glass and make contact with the guide on the other side. In this *Simple Guide to Judaism* I have tried to present this opportunity to you. The pages that follow are not intended to provide an objective study of texts and artifacts, but rather a subjective exploration of the things which make me a Jew. I hope that through this shared exploration you will come to a shared appreciation of the Jewish world as I perceive it.

Hebrew words have been transliterated into vowels and consonants which have their standard English pronunciation. While Hebrew has acquired different regional pronunciations (particularly noticeable between the Ashkenazim and Sephardim), modern Hebrew has been used (which incidentally coincides with Sephardic pronunciation). Note that the letters 'ch' are pronounced as in the Scottish 'loch'. In modern Hebrew the last syllable is normally stressed.

I have used the English word 'God' when referring to the Creator, despite that fact that this word has acquired many connotations in English which do not necessarily match the Hebrew. By the way, in Hebrew 'God' is a masculine noun and I have therefore used He and His: this should be interpreted neither as an anthropomorphism nor as gender-biased language.

Many people have helped me assemble this short guide. The gratitude which I owe to my master and teacher Rabbi Boruch Epstein, of blessed memory, is impossible to quantify. His presence is as direct now as it was when I first met him a quarter of a century ago. I thank my friends and colleagues Rabbi Nosson Geisler and Rabbi Dr Menachem Gordon, who reviewed sections of this text. Their advice was invaluable, and any errors which remain, or any imperfections in implementing their suggestions, are mine alone.

I also thank my editor and publisher Paul Norbury for his editorial skill, enthusiasm and decisiveness in this project. Nina, my wife, and our children have provided encouragement and suggestions for which I am most grateful. Finally, I would like to thank you, the reader: without you I could not have written and without you I could not serve as a guide.

DAVID STARR-GLASS
Jerusalem

Chapter 1

What is Judaism?

Who are Jews? What is Judaism? These questions are entwined, and in that intertwining there is a great deal of latitude for confusion. In a more perfect world a Jew should be one who believes and practises the tenets of Judaism: there should be an alignment between the who and the what. However, in a less than perfect world, there is an inevitable slippage between ethnic identity and religious conviction. This slippage can make it very difficult for the non-Jewish observer to understand the essential aspects of both being a Jew and practising Judaism.

Let us begin with a more general question. If Jews are part of humanity, and if Judaism is part of a mosaic of world religions, what (from a Jewish perspective) is the purpose of humanity at large – of Creation?

Jewish View of Creation

The traditional Jewish understanding of the Creation is that God brought the universe into existence and created primordial Man (Adam) and

⊙ *The Star of David – two triangles symbolizing the balance of the universe, found on medieval Kabbalistic amulets*

Woman (Eve, or Chava). His creation was aware of Him and had the ability to relate to Him. However, they were also conscious of their own, not necessarily congruent, desires and agendas: they were created with free will. God desired a symmetry of love and responsibility but His children could not enter into this relationship and became alienated from Him. Later, the progeny of Adam and Eve – humanity as a whole – grew more distanced from their source of being. Increasingly, they saw a fragmented world with separated powers and forces. They lost a sensitivity for the oneness of their Creator and for their unity within Him.

Jewish tradition accepts that Abraham (Avraham), the son of an idol-maker, saw the transcending unity of God in spite of the idolatry that surrounded him in his native Charan, a city in northern Mesopotamia, in what is now southeast Turkey near the border with Syria. This happened about three-and-a-half thousand years ago. Abraham and his wife, Sarah, set out first to explore, then to proclaim, a religion of unity. Abraham practised many of the precepts of what was to become Judaism, and while God did enter into an enduring Covenant with him and his descendants there was, as yet, no distinct Jewish nation. For instance, the descendants of Abraham's son, Ishamael, were later to form the Semitic (but non-Jewish) tribes that would later proclaim a different approach to monotheism: Islam.

Only one of Abraham's children followed in the spiritual tradition of his father. In turn, only one of Isaac's children continued on Abraham's path. Guided and nurtured by God, Jacob (also known as Israel) brought all his children to the threshold of a new, spiritually centred nationhood. Until now there had been many individuals who had seen and proclaimed Godliness; however, there was no people dedicated to that purpose. The children of Jacob went down into Egypt where they were purified through slavery and poverty. The exile in Egypt is

⊙ *Semitic tribesman, c. 1800 BCE, in traditional dress, leads a bull to ritual slaughter. Detail from a wall painting in the palace at Mari on the Euphrates*

likened to an iron crucible used to refine gold: the impurities in the molten gold were absorbed by the red-hot iron walls. The extended family was starting to be fused into a unified people.

⊙ *An archeologist-artist's impression of a scene in a Canaanite household, based on the findings of a family tomb in Jericho, c. 1500 BCE.*

At the darkest moment of their exile, the remnants of Jacob's family were openly and miraculously wrenched out from their anguish. As free individuals – but more significantly as a newly created nation – this first Jewish generation proclaimed that they would both keep and comprehend the Torah (the Five Books of Moses – p. 24) which was given at Mount Sinai. These commitments were irrevocable. The Jewish nation was bound in an eternal covenant to its liberator and reconnected with its Creator.

Birth of a New Religion and Nation

The birth of a new religion (Judaism), as well as the birth of a new nation (the Jewish people), took place at Mount Sinai. From the perspective of most Jewish commentators, the nation of Israel is unique and enjoys its special intimacy with God only if the Jews adhere to the precepts of the Torah. The nation of Israel does not see itself as inherently superior or privileged. Rather, Jews see themselves as bound in a service of perfection which has serious responsibilities, sublime rewards and significant consequences.

To be a Jew, that is to have lineage within the house of Israel, is to have a potential to enter into the service of perfection which goes on between the Jewish nation and its Creator. To be a Jew is not, as has often been remarked, to have the word stamped on your passport: it is to have the ability to light lamps in a darkened world. Belonging to the people of Israel means, ultimately, being in possession of a soul (a *neshama*) which is in tune with the Torah.

Souls cannot be examined, so how can one tell if a particular person is in possession of a Jewish soul? The Rabbis have taught that the children of a Jewish woman, irrespective of the father, will possess Jewish souls and will be regarded as Jews. It makes no difference whether the woman was religiously observant or even ignorant that she was herself Jewish. The people of Israel is a community of similar and specially attuned souls.

❯❯ 'The Lamp-lighter'

A Jew may intellectually renounce his Jewish identity, but it is considered that he cannot alter the state of his *neshama*, or, ultimately, his spiritual identity. Even Jews who are far from participating in religious observance are spiritually connected with the people of the nation of Israel and have the potential to return. As the late Rabbi Yosef Itzchak Schneerson remarked: A Jew is a lamp-lighter. The light is never extinguished.

Who Can Become a Jew?

Non-Jews often ask whether someone outside the people of Israel can enter into Judaism. Judaism is a non-proselytizing religion which advises non-Jews to live ethically and in peace and harmony with God. It recognizes the value of the righteous of the other nations and neither requires, nor advocates, that such righteous people embrace Judaism. Converts to Judaism (Hebrew: *gerai tzeddek* – righteous strangers) are generally discouraged. They are accepted only if an authorized religious court recognizes in them an unrevealed *neshama*: the process of conversion is in essence the process of exposing a hidden Jewish connection.

The prospective convert must come without any ulterior motives. The desire to marry a Jew, for example, is such an ulterior motive and would not by itself constitute grounds for a valid conversion. If would-be converts are motivated by love of God, they may petition a competent rabbinical court and seek conversion. The prospective converts will inevitably be rejected on the initial three or four petitions, but if they persist, and if their petitions are considered to be motivated only by the highest desires, then the rabbinical court may accept them.

The Torah

What the convert accepts – and what all Jews are capable of accepting – is the Torah. The Torah is often compared to the blueprint of the universe; it came before the Creation and it came before humanity. The word 'Torah', which might be translated as 'instruction', means in its broadest sense the totality of what is knowable about God's relationship with the universe. In a more narrow sense the word 'Torah' is used for the *chumash*, the Five Books of Moses – Genesis, Exodus, Leviticus, Numbers and Deuteronomy. These five books are in turn often known as the Pentateuch (Greek: five books). In this guide we will use 'Torah' when describing the totality of Jewish knowledge about this God relationship; *Sefer Torah* when referring to the parchment scroll on which the Five Books are written, and *chumash* for the printed version of the same.

Within the Jewish understanding of Creation,

symmetry is considered to be significant. Opposite, and complementary, elements in the universe were paired together. It is said that the Torah (given a female embodiment in Jewish tradition) complained to God that she had no partner; she was isolated by her uniqueness. For her, He revealed the souls of the children of Israel and joined them in an eternal union. Even before creation, He had decided to single out a nation who would be responsible for proclaiming and sustaining the relationship between God and His Creation. The rabbinical dictum states that the final outcome (the formation of the Jewish people and their receiving of the Torah) was envisaged in His original thought (of creating the universe).

The Essence of Jewish Belief

But what is the essence of this Torah which the Jewish people are heir to? Firstly, let us recognize that there is within Judaism an inherent tension which has been expressed in many ways. On the one hand Judaism prescribes – often in great detail – rules of behaviour, prohibitions, detailed ritual and formulae for personal and societal conduct: the thrust might be construed as narrow and legalistic. On the other hand, Judaism promotes – in the same amount of detail – ethical reflection, consideration and respect in relationships, and the development of sensitivities which resonate with our modern, and post-modern, experience: an

⊙ The short ceremony of kiddush *takes place at the onset of the* Shabbat *(Friday evening) and on Saturday morning; it is a simple dedication of the day, performed over a cup of wine*

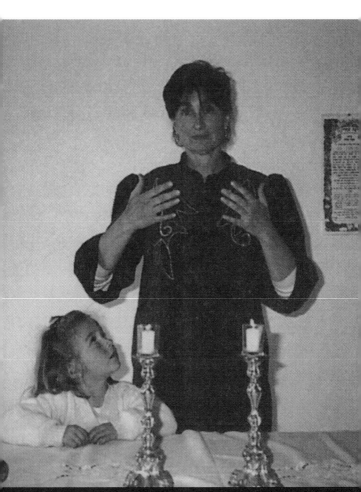

⊙ Shabbat *is welcomed into the Jewish home by the wife. She lights a minimum of two candles, symbolic of the two central aspects: 'remembering' and 'keeping' the holiness of the day*

emphasis on the contemplative and the spiritual. It seems unresolved as to whether the essential demands made on the Jew are legalistic or spiritual in nature.

Let us consider, for a moment, the Jewish understanding of the *Shabbat*, the seventh, sabbatical day which is dedicated to God. Does one focus on keeping the minutiae of the laws pertaining to *Shabbat*, or does one emphasize enjoying the exhilaration of the day? For the observant Jew the answer is transparently obvious: one does both. There is an explicit Torah dimension of 'keeping' (which stresses boundaries for behaviour) and of 'remembering' (which emphasizes the internal emotional aspects) within the day. These dimensions may be considered as being in tension, but they are also seen as being equally essential and fundamentally unified.

» Quest for Balance

Much of Judaism is the quest for balance. The balanced Jew is neither the one who mindlessly follows the letter of the law, nor the one who wishes only to follow its nebulous spirit. On the lower slopes of Mount Sinai the Jewish people were wed to their Torah. At that time they asserted: We shall do, and we shall understand. .

Consider the Torah prohibition against wearing '*shatnez*'. This law prohibits the wearing of mixtures of wool and linen fibres. This prohibition is given without an explicit reason: why can we not mix these two fibres together? Side by side with this prohibition is the central, positive commandment of loving one's neighbour as oneself. This seems much more attuned with our understanding of what is right and what is wrong.

Ostensibly, these two commandments are sharply contrasted in terms of perceived content and emotional engagement. One seems distant and without obvious reason. The other seems almost intuitive. Yet Judaism sees each commandment as expressing different unique and mystical ideas: both are equally valid. There can be no preferences, options or choices at either an intellectual or an emotional level. There is no relativity within Torah expression. Ideas of relativity – close/far, internal/external, inclusive/exclusive – are not relevant within Torah thought, even though we each have our own personal preferences and viewpoints.

External Expression v. Internal Appreciation

This preference of seeing Judaism as a religion either of external expression or of internal appreciation has resulted in obvious tensions within the community of Jews. It has also been perplexing for the non-Jewish observer. In the early history of Judaism, the expression of the message promulgated at Mount Sinai was shaped by a succession of prophets. Each of these stressed an under-appreciated value or an under-performed requirement. All of them were regarded as out of step with their time and society. However, this process of ongoing, divine input seems to have been directed to a definite goal: to produce a sharper appreciation of the subtle equilibrium between thought and deed which characterizes the Jewish heritage.

Judaism is a religion neither of doing nor of thinking: it is a faith where both are accorded equal weight. Judaism lays equal stress on fulfilling all Torah precepts. Although some are obscure and very difficult to fathom intellectually (like *shatnez*), and although others seem intuitive and appealing (like loving one's neighbour), all commandments are incumbent on the Jew. For many there is a tension in Jewish perceptions of mission. There is also, however, an ongoing dynamic of faith which pushes the Jewish community closer to a sense of equilibrium: sometimes stressing the legalistic, sometimes stressing the ethical.

Chapter 2

Brief History of Judaism

Judaism has a history which spans more than three-and-a-half thousand years, yet it would be wrong to regard it as an old religion. As a revealed expression of God's will it is beyond time: eternally valid rather than old-fashioned or modern. The expression of Judaism has, of course, changed throughout time with the changing internal and external environments of the Jewish nation.

The Temple

The Jewish people wandered for forty years in the desert after they were rescued from Egypt. During that period they began to engage in an elaborate, symbolic pattern of worship. The centre of this worship was a moveable temple – the *mishkan*, or Tabernacle – which Moses was instructed to build. When they entered the land of Israel, the *mishkan* was moved from location to location until it was eventually set up in Jerusalem. In time, a permanent structure was erected in Jerusalem (the First Temple) and this became the spiritual centre of the Jewish people.

⊙ Judean exiles (two women, two girls and a man leading an ox cart) forced out of their home city of Lachish by the Assyrian tyrant Sennacherib, c. 700 BCE. Detail of a bas-relief panel of the period

The First Temple was destroyed in 586 BCE by the Babylonians. Following its destruction the Jewish nation was taken into captivity in Babylon, although they were eventually permitted to return and rebuild it as the Second Temple, also in Jerusalem. This Second Temple was eventually destroyed by the Romans in the year 70 of the Common Era. While a Third Temple has been promised, to date there are no prophetic signs concerning its restoration. Today, Jews still consider the Temple Mount in Jerusalem to be the holiest place in the world. The site is also holy to Islam (Jerusalem is their third most holy city) and it is presently covered by a complex of mosques.

Temple Sacrifice

The Temple concept, with the related sacrifices (*korbanot*) which were performed there, is difficult for many modern Jews to understand. The first difficulty, perhaps, is in the use of the word 'sacrifice'. It is important to understand that the connotation which this word has within contemporary, Western culture is quite different from that inferred by Judaism.

⊙ *A tenth-century BCE limestone altar from the Israelite city of Megido, similar to the one described in the Book of Kings*

» Sacrifice – *Korban*

The Hebrew word to describe sacrifice is *korban*, which indicates a drawing close. The *korban* was a specified act which allowed either the individual or the community as a whole to draw close to God. These carefully specified acts, the circumstances of which are minutely detailed in the Torah, opened windows of divine connection. It was through these windows that atonement, joy, thanksgiving and the fulfilment of promises were all expressed.

The specific *korban* which had to be brought is detailed in the Torah. Cattle, goats, sheep and pigeons might be brought and sacrificed within the Temple precincts. Similarly flour, oil and incense could be brought, depending on the specific requirements which the Torah indicated. Sometimes the offering was consumed by fire in the Temple; sometimes specified parts of the offering were eaten by the *cohanim* (page 117); sometimes (as in the case of the Pascal lamb) the flesh was returned to the person bringing the offering for consumption at home.

The *korban* incorporated the physical dimensions of time and place. The time when the sacrifice could be brought, eaten or burned was very precise. The place where they could be sacrificed, eaten or burned was equally limited. If the *korban* was consummated within these windows of opportunity, it was effective and a divine connection was made.

If time and place did not come together, the sacrifice could, paradoxically, defile and harm.

With the destruction of the Second Temple the institution of temple worship came to an end: in practice, sacrifices are no longer performed. The Talmudic tractates dealing with temple sacrifice are still widely studied and are alluded to in contemporary ritual.

Incidentally, the modern synagogue is not a 'Temple' (even though the word is used by non-Orthodox communities) but a place of worship. Many commentators indicate that the Temple which was destroyed in Jerusalem was replaced by the 'temple' within a person – the heart being the altar, etc.

Exile

It was not only the temple service which ceased with the destruction of the Second Temple: the Jewish nation was dispersed. In exile they recognized the potential danger of their estranged position and ultimately moved towards recording the vast amount of Torah learning which had been preserved as an oral tradition.

This was the time of the compilation of the Babylonian Talmud (completed by about the sixth century CE). Academies of Jewish learning flourished. The evolving aspiration of the Jewish

Diaspora communities became the active acquisition of Torah knowledge. 'Diaspora' (Greek: scattered seed) communities were those which developed in exile, outside the land of Israel. These communities responded to two significant issues: (i) the challenge of preserving the customs and spiritual learning of the past, and (ii) the demands of living in an alien and ever-changing world.

As different Jewish communities mixed with other civilizations, changes of emphasis began to appear within these communities. Thus, within the communities of Spain an infusion of classical Greek and contemporary Moslem philosophy shaped the intellectual output of many great Jewish thinkers. The Rambam – the acronym for Rabbi Moshe ben Maimon, also known as Maimonides – in his monumental *Mishneh Torah*, written in the tenth century CE, classified and teased out the intricate fabric of the Talmud. He categorized this vast work in terms of the Aristotelian philosophy with which he was conversant, making Jewish learning accessible to a wider and less erudite readership. He emphasized an intellectual approach to the source, structure and implications of the *mitzvot*, rather than placing a heavier metaphysical emphasis on their acceptance and performance. He and his community were able to uphold an authentic Jewish heritage while being fully involved with the modernity of their age (the Rambam was a renowned physician).

» *Mitzvot*

Learning about a sacred activity, which could no longer be done, was now understood to be almost the same as doing it. The *mitzvot* (commandments) associated with the land of Israel and the Temple were now no longer possible for the exiles, and an intellectual parallelism was substituted. The goal was to preserve that knowledge which had been an active ingredient of Jewish practice and life. This retention of Jewish knowledge was to be a hallmark of the Jewish people. Identity and continuity were now the key issues which had to be addressed.

The Jews in Europe

The Rambam lived at the end of the so-called Golden Age of Spanish Jewry. During that period there was considerable intellectual activity and growth within the mutual respect between Jews and non-Jews. This, however, was not typical of the Jewish experience in Europe. Over the next several hundred years the rest of Europe was overtaken by subsequent waves of Crusade fervour, crisis within the Catholic Church, the growth of the Lutheran reforms, and a nascent intellectual enlightenment. Most of these historic milestones were marked by trauma and pain in the Jewish communities of Europe. If it was not rabid anti-Semitism, then it was forced conversion to Christianity, or the wholesale massacre of Jewish communities.

These communities shared common homelands with their neighbours. They also shared, some might claim, a common spiritual heritage. And yet this was neither the time nor the place for communality. In England for example, in the wake of Crusade fervour, five hundred Jewish men, women and children were massacred at York in 1190. But it was not simply religious hysteria which caused their death; it was also, paradoxically, the common spiritual heritage which they shared with their Christian brothers.

Jews, for instance, followed a Torah precept not to take interest on a monetary loan made to 'a brother'. Christians had taken upon themselves the same commandment. For a Christian to borrow money he needed a Jewish financier, for the Jew was certainly not his scriptural brother. The field of banking was one of the few things which Jews could engage in: they were prohibited from attending universities and from practising most professions.

For the Diaspora Jew there is still a sense of hurt that the spiritual heritage which Christians might have claimed to share was used to alienate and distance Jews in Christian society. But it was not simply alienation which the English communities had to put up with. They were forcibly expelled from England in 1290, and only returned cautiously in the days of Cromwell and his Commonwealth.

Christianity and Judaism

At this point it may be appropriate to mention briefly the effect of Christ and Christianity on Judaism. The birth, life and crucifixion of Jesus seems from contemporary sources to have had little impact on the Jewish nation. In general, it was a time of tension and oppression. As is becoming increasingly appreciated among Christian scholars, Jesus behaved in a profoundly Jewish way. His teachings are quite in tune with contemporary rabbinical notions. Indeed, the flavour of the Sermon on the Mount is quite similar to the ethical teachings in the Chapters of the Fathers (*Mishna*, tractate *Avot*).

It was not Jesus who had an effect on Judaism: rather it was the Christian Church, in both its original and reformed expressions. Perhaps the greatest tragedy in the painful relationship between the Jews and the Church was the early Church's holding on too long to the notion that Jesus was, in fact, the Jewish messiah. Had Christianity set out as a new religious expression, divorced from what had gone before, perhaps things might have been different. The insistence on a 'common' Jewish source needlessly complicated matters for the Church and for the Jewish people. It led to repression, missionary campaigns, forced conversion and institutional violence in the form of the pogrom. The pain and bitterness of the past two thousand years of Christian-Jewish interaction is something to which most Jews are acutely sensitive.

New Movements and Thinkers

The history of almost all Jewish communities in Europe is painful. Persecution was met with fortitude; deportation and pogrom with tearful resignation. Under such circumstances many began seeing Judaism in terms of providing redemption and an ultimate messianic age. These were very old ideas, but they now were seen as central. While not expressed in all Jewish communities, there were significant moves towards a mystical abstraction (or escapism) in the study of *Merkava* mysticism, or the Kabbala (Hebrew: received knowledge). There was also much enthusiasm for short-lived pseudo-messianic cults like that of Shabbatai Tzvi (1626–76).

There was a widespread move towards Chassidism, which provided a mystical world vision that stressed love and kindness. The movement was founded by the Ba'al Shem Tov (Israel ben Eliezer, 1700–60) and spread rapidly in Central and Eastern Europe. This movement stressed the sanctity and authority of a *rebbe* (a personal spiritual leader) and a mystical interpretation of scripture.

The erosion of community strength and of religious authority was particularly apparent during the period of the Enlightenment (eighteenth century) when a secular shift to rationality and humanism was enthusiastically adopted by many Jews. The move seemed to be towards a liberal, and liberating, world of common humanity and egalitarianism. Distinction between Jew and non-Jew, a yearning for wider social responsibility and the allegiance owed to one's country of birth were significant issues. Jewish thinkers and activists were often to the front of these trans-European movements.

The effect of the Enlightenment was most pronounced in Western Europe (France, and what is now Germany) and led to a fundamental reappraisal by many of what was seen to be the underlying exclusivity of Judaism. Exclusivity was seen to be the main cause of exclusion from contemporary non-Jewish society.

Against this background there was within many Western European communities the desire to reform existing Jewish practice. It is probably more accurate to see this as a sociological accommodation to an excluding external culture (German, Danish, English, etc.), rather than a theological movement. The reformers wanted to reduce the high and distinctive profile which they saw as separating them. Circumcision, *Shabbat* observance, *kashrut* and indeed most traditional Jewish practices were jettisoned. Prayer-book references to a messianic age, or to a Jewish national goal, were erased. Services were conducted in the local language, and some even celebrated what was left of *Shabbat* on Sunday and imported pipe organs into their synagogues. It is hard not to recognize a desperate – and an understandable – longing to reduce all cultural difference and behave exactly like the dominant Christian community.

Pressures for Assimilation

Traditional Judaism in Western Europe was challenged by these massive pressures for assimilation. Rabbi Shimshon Rafael Hirsch (1808–88) put forward a vigorous defence of Jewish norms. He stressed the profoundly symbolic element within Jewish practice, particularly in areas such as Temple worship. Hirsch, an exceptional Jewish scholar and member of the Austrian parliament, developed a modern, Orthodox bulwark against the assimilationism of the Reform movements. By contrast, in Eastern Europe the main spiritual force was exerted by Rabbi Moshe Sofer of Pressburg (The Chatam Sofer, 1763–1839) who took a rigid 'what-is-new-is-forbidden' approach. His message lacked intellectual or emotional persuasion, but then opportunity for assimilation was more severely constrained in the East.

Economic pressures caused substantial population changes in the distribution of world Jewry. North America understandably presented the illusion of a '*golden medina*' (Yiddish: golden land) and the emigration of large numbers of impoverished Eastern European Jews created a growing population of people alienated from both their old and new cultures. Central and Eastern Europe had not been a homogeneous camp of Orthodox values; however, these communities had retained a conservative religious profile because of external forces and internal authority. In America external and internal restraints were eroded. In America Judaism was an ethnic, rather than religious, expression. It was also shaped by pluralism, diversity and the notion of the cultural melting pot.

Challenges of the Twentieth Century

Starting in the 1930s, in Germany, a new and grotesque eruption of virulent anti-Semitism started to spread over Europe. The magnitude and trauma of the Holocaust (1939–45) is difficult to come to terms with. It left a third of world Jewry butchered and reduced to ash. It destroyed European communities which had existed for a thousand years. In its wake the impetus for a regained national homeland was unstoppable.

The State of Israel came into being on 5 May 1948 and became a place of safety and hope for millions of Jewish immigrants from all over the world.

The State of Israel, where today one-third of world Jewry live, has been in existence for almost sixty years. During that time the views of both Israelis and Diaspora communities about Israel have changed. Originally, the political founders of Israel saw it as a secular, socialist state which could be cut adrift from a painful history of humiliation. It was to be a place for Jewish expression and freedom. However, the country has been challenged not only by external threats and wars, but also by growing dissent and frustration. Secular Israelis resent the coercive bureaucracy of the State's religious institution, particularly the rabbinical courts. Religious Israelis bemoan the lack of traditional Jewish values among the young. The schism between secular and religious Israelis has grown ever wider; the rhetoric has become more inflamed. Diaspora communities now no longer look to the Israel experience as a salvation for cultural Jewishness or relevant Judaism.

» Heritage and Identity

In the Diaspora, Judaism is confronting the same problems which all minority religions are facing. Unprecedented assimilation, marriage with non-Jews (often exceeding 50%) and low fertility rates have led to shrinking communities, unsure of their survival, let alone their heritage. Yet survival for Jews, in a non-Jewish world, is always an issue of heritage and identity; heritage and identity are always issues of knowledge and faith. Education is a central feature of Judaism, and many communities are exploring new, more relevant approaches to gaining knowledge and insight into their Jewish experience.

There are more Jewish resources available now than ever before. All major Jewish texts are available in English translation, often enriched by well researched material culled from the last thousand years of Jewish scholarship. An increasing number of Jews are trying to acquire the Hebrew language skills necessary to deal with original sources; you cannot really appreciate Judaism without Hebrew. Many spend time after work in private or communal learning groups. Many listen to Talmud discourses on tape-recorders as they commute to work. Each day tens of thousands of Jews throughout the world sit down to learn the same page of the Talmud; they complete the whole work in seven years. Local

Jewish day schools, rabbinical colleges (*yeshivot*) and individual rabbis have initiated a web of outreach programmes, bringing a new religious dimension to Jews who were not particularly interested or inspired by their Judaism.

Chapter 3

Aims & Teachings

Jewish Vision of the Future

When, almost two thousand years ago, a prospective convert asked the sage Hillel the Elder to explain the basic centrality of Judaism, he received the following answer: Do not do unto others that which you yourself would find hateful. In a similar time, and under similar circumstances, Rabbi Akiva suggested that the central rule in the Torah is to love your neighbour as yourself.

Both of these rabbinic authorities had been placed in the dilemma of having to provide a concise, off-the-cuff answer. What they stressed is that in spite of the detail and the clutter of Jewish religious requirements there is a broad sense of direction. It points towards understanding, reconciliation and love. This broad position transcends the Jewish nation. It involves all the nations of the world, indeed all of creation. In this broadest sense, Judaism represents a covenant between God and all His created world, in which the people of Israel are the instrument through which contact and communication is to be established.

⊙ The Shrine of the Book houses the Dead Sea Scrolls at the Israel Museum, Jerusalem. On display in the centre is the 24-foot long scroll of Isaiah

❯❯ 'Liberating the Light'

Consider a metaphor used by the Kabbalists: The service of the Jewish people is to sift through the pieces of the vessels which were shattered when the supernal Light was placed in them. The world is a place of *tikkun* (Hebrew: repair), of restoration and of ongoing perfection. The world is seen as a place of broken shards, with sparks of supernal Light attached to them, and obscured by them. The ultimate purpose of the Jewish people is to search out, to assemble and to liberate these sparks, wherever they may be found.

In this aspect Judaism is universal, with a message and a mission for all of the world. However, there is no notion that the rest of the world must be forced into accepting a Jewish vision of the future. The rest of the world is to see – by looking at the Jewish people – that there is something unique, enduring and tenacious in their faith, and in the object of their love. The Jewish people are to pose a perpetual question, rather than provide a facile answer.

Jews believe in the eventual arrival of the Messiah (Hebrew: *mashiach*, the anointed), who will herald a new age of communication between the Creator and His creation. It is unclear exactly what this era will be like, but all are agreed that it will be strikingly obvious when it does eventually come. Before the creation there was a unity within God; with the coming of the Messiah there may well be a similar return to such an undivided unity.

Mitzvot: The Jewish Commandments

Each Jew is responsible for fulfilling the commandments which God gave: this is how purpose is defined and measured. To perform a *mitzva* (singular) is to engage in a process which has repercussions beyond the physical world which we inhabit. To be offered the opportunity to perform a *mitzva* is considered the ultimate act of love which God can give the Jewish soul. It was for this reason that the Jewish people were entrusted with an inordinate number of *mitzvot*, as many, it is said, as the seeds of a pomegranate.

Tradition has established that there is a total of 613 commandments, made up of 248 affirmative commandments and 365 prohibitions. Jewish learning explains that all of these *mitzvot* are derived from the first two utterances of the Ten Commandments (page 50). All of the affirmative commandments have their source in the first commandment (I Am), while the negative ones are rooted in the second (You shall have no other gods).

While there are a total of 613 *mitzvot* many of these had to do with temple practices and have been redundant since the destruction of the Temple. It is estimated that there are only between sixty and seventy *mitzvot* which can be performed in our times, and even then some of these are unique to those who inhabit the land of Israel.

» The Ten Commandments

Perhaps the most widely known set of *mitzvot* are those which were received by Moses, at Mount Sinai – the Ten Commandments. While these were given in a spectacularly dramatic way, they represent only one set – not the summation – of the 613 commandments which the Torah contains (Exodus 20: 1-17).

1. I am the Lord your God who brought you out from the land of Egypt, out from the house of bondage.

2. You shall have no other gods before me. You shall not make any representation or image of anything which is in the heavens above, or in the earth below, or in the waters which are under the earth. You shall not bow down to them nor serve them, for I the Lord your God am a God who demands exclusivity, rendering the sins of the fathers to their children for the third and fourth generation of those who hate me, and showing loving kindness to the thousandth generation of those who love me and keep My commandments.

3. You shall not take the name of the Lord God in vain, for the Lord will not hold a person guiltless if he uses His name in vain.

4. Remember the *Shabbat* to keep it holy. Six days you shall labour and do all of your work but the seventh day shall be a *Shabbat* for the Lord God. You shall not do any work, neither you nor your son, nor your daughter, nor your servant, nor your maid, nor your cattle nor the stranger who is within your gates. For in six days the Lord made the heavens, and the earth, and the sea and all that is in them, and rested on the seventh day. Therefore the Lord blessed the *Shabbat* and sanctified it.

5. Honour your father and your mother so that your days on the
   earth, which the Lord your God gave you, shall
   be lengthened.

6. Do not murder.

7. Do not commit adultery.

8. Do not steal.

9. Do not testify falsely against your neighbour.

10. Do not covet your neighbour's house: do not covet his wife,
    nor his servants, nor his maids, nor his ox, nor his ass, nor
    anything which is your neighbour's.

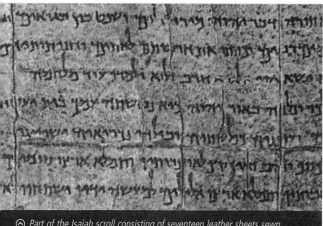

⊙ *Part of the Isaiah scroll consisting of seventeen leather sheets sewn
together, on which are fifty-four columns of text*

It is important to keep in mind that *mitzvot* are not simply warm, fuzzy good deeds. They transcend knowledge and intellect, even though many rational explanations have been attributed to most of them at some time or another. For example, the cosmic impact of eating pig meat is indeterminable. Ultimately, pork is not eaten for one reason only: it is prohibited by the Torah.

Principles of Faith

Paradoxically, while dissension and genuine matters of disagreement abound among Jewish scholars, there is little dogma. Thus, in the time of the *Mishna*, the earliest surviving work of rabbinic literature (see page 100), there were substantial differences between the rulings of the rabbinical dynasties of Hillel and Shamai. Among other things they disagreed on the ritual purity of vessels and on laws relating to marriage. Notwithstanding such differences, we learn that they borrowed vessels from one another and that their families married into one another. These disagreements were 'in the name of Heaven', and were not based on narrower, individual or societal concerns. Diversity, within the overall framework of accepted Jewish concepts, had always been permissible.

While disagreements are common, Judaism, under the systemizing influence of Christianity, has made several attempts at defining just what it is that Jews believe. Such a listing of the Principles of Faith may help define normative Jewish belief, but it should not be thought of as restricting or limiting. Indeed, just because of such a restriction (limiting normative Jewish belief to less than the whole Torah), many authorities have been very wary about attempts to produce such creeds. Likewise, while observant Jews will usually subscribe to such a list they may vary in their levels of intensity of commitment to specific items.

The most famous listing was made by Moses Maimonides, the Rambam. He itemized thirteen articles which he considered absolutely incumbent upon every Jew: (i) God created everything; (ii) He is perfect unity; (iii) He is non-corporate; (iv) He is first and last; (v) He alone can be prayed to; (vi) the words of the Prophets are true; (vii) Moshe (Moses) is the greatest of the Prophets; (viii) the Torah is true in totality; (ix) the Torah is immutable; (x) God knows our thoughts and deeds; (xi) there are rewards and punishments; (xii) the Messiah will come; (xiii) there will be a resurrection of the dead.

Such articles of faith are meant to assist the Jew's spiritual quest. Acceptance, rejection or scepticism are personal issues. If a person does not approach the enactment of a commandment in a positive manner, this results in the loss of an opportunity to connect with a higher level of God awareness and, with only two exceptions, there is no penalty for that other than the loss of the opportunity itself. Transgression of negative commandments may lead to a penalty; however, these days there is no rabbinical/legal apparatus which deals with these infractions. Such penalties are, for the most part, no longer in our hands. Wilful transgressions are an issue between the perpetrator and what Jews refer to as the 'heavenly court'.

» Different Jewish Groupings

In discussing creeds it is perhaps important to distinguish between words like 'Orthodox', 'Ultra-Orthodox', 'Modern Orthodox', 'Conservative', 'Traditional' and 'Reform' as applied to what Jews believe and what they do. A central tenet of Judaism is that the Jewish people are unified. However, in reality, they do things in many different ways, much to the annoyance of other Jews and the confusion of non-Jews. There is simply no theological justification for dividing Jews, or for Jews dividing themselves, into such groupings. What lies between the apparent variants of Judaism is what is accepted as the word of God, how this interpreted and how it is responded to.

There are obvious cultural differences between the black-hatted, black-coated Ultra-Orthodox rabbi and the clean-shaven, bare-headed Reform rabbi. They will act differently on *Shabbat*, and they will act differently on a Monday morning as well. They will undoubtedly have a different image of self and of one another. They may even think differently. Nevertheless, however different they are, the fact is they are also both Jews. I would suggest that they are separated culturally and socially much more than they are theologically.

Chapter 4

Festivals

It would be inaccurate to think of Jewish festivals
purely as celebrations of the past. Instead, it would
be more correct to see them as recurring moments
of particular awareness of a certain experience. It is
as though the dimension of time is punctuated by a
cycle of celebrations which, while capturing the
essence of a historic past, also express a relevant
present and an embryonic future. In Jewish
thought, time is considered to be like a helix: in
passing through time we encounter zones of
meaning (festivals), which we have encountered in
the past and which we will encounter in the future.

The basis for all major festivals is to be found
in the Torah. There they are enumerated and
succinctly described. Layers of meaning and
significance have accreted over the past
thousands of years, giving each festival a set of
rich and unique flavours. The festivals have
multiple dimensions – historical, agricultural,
social, nationalistic, symbolic, mystical – each
reflecting the different stages of collective
thought, condition and vision which the Jewish
people have passed through.

⊙ Children are central to the Jewish family, and the Jewish family is central to Judaism. Here children anticipate the coming Shabbat, which is usually a day which celebrates the family

Shabbat

The most important of these festivals is the
weekly observance of *Shabbat* – the seventh day
of creation. Of *Shabbat* it has been said that it has
kept the Jewish people more than they have kept
it: it serves to bind the Jewish people to their
heritage at an individual, family and community
level. *Shabbat* provides a steady pulse of religious
energy and renewal. Observance of *Shabbat* is
taken as a prime requirement of normative Jewish
life. *Shabbat* begins on Friday at sunset (all
Jewish days begin at sunset) and extends through
until Saturday evening.

In the Ten Commandments, there are two
injunctions: 'to keep' and 'to remember' *Shabbat*.
These are taken as referring to (i) the constraints
and (ii) the possibilities which are unique to that
day. It is significant that the constraints which
mark the day are derived from the work done in
constructing and operating the Tabernacle
(*mishkan*). The *mishkan*, which was constructed
in the desert immediately after the exodus from
Egypt, was to serve as a place of spiritual
meeting. The *mishkan* was brought into being so
that God should have, as it says in the mystical
writings, 'a dwelling-place in both upper and
lower worlds': a dwelling-place within the
congregation of Israel.

Construction of the *mishkan* was an exercise in bringing down the Divine presence, yet all of these constructive efforts were suspended at the onset of *shabbat*. This suggests that encounters with the Divine can take place within the real world which surrounds us, and is not restricted to a unique, designated place. It also suggests that the sanctuary within time (*Shabbat*) is indestructible, and takes precedence over the sanctuary in space (the Temple) which was destroyed.

On *Shabbat* the observant Jew will refrain from a total of thirty-nine categories of productive work – planting, reaping, construction, cooking, etc. – and derivatives of those categories. The issue is not one of resting, or of limiting physical exertion, or indeed of work in its usual sense. What is being recognized is that human ingenuity and creativity, which were used to make God's very sanctuary on earth, are limited and ineffectual in the absorbing presence of God, which fills the day. God Himself rested on the *Shabbat*. On that day He was unified with His creation.

These constraints on constructive activities provide an external boundary which delimit an inner space. It is this inner space which can then be filled with the positive opportunities of *Shabbat*: inviting guests to one's home; sharing meals with family and friends; improving the harmony between family members; spending more time in prayer and study.

The noun *Shabbat* can be either masculine or feminine, but the feminine sense is usually taken. She will be treated as a beloved and honoured guest: as a bride – as a queen. Before she arrives everyone bathes and dresses in their best clothes. The home has been thoroughly cleaned. Candles have been placed on the table and will be lit to greet her. Extra courses will be served at the family meal in her honour.

As the sun sets on Friday afternoon people assemble in synagogues and sing to welcome the queen/bride:

> Come, my dear friend, call out to the Bride;
> Let us accept the presence of *Shabbat*.
> Observe and remember were in that
>   single utterance,
> Which the indivisible God caused us to hear.
> God is one and His Name is one:
> We can call on Him, and beautify Him, and
>   praise Him . . .
>
> RABBI SHLOMO HALEVI ALKABETZ (16th century)

The idea of personifying and welcoming the *Shabbat* developed within the Jewish mystical tradition of the sixteenth century. There, the advent of the queen/bride was seen in terms of a passionate spiritual union. This beautiful and intense imagery is reflected in the prayer book:

> My soul's beloved, Father of compassion,
> Draw Your servant to Your will.
> Then Your servant will run like a gazelle
> To prostrate himself in Your presence.
> Your companionship will be to him like
> Honey dripping from the comb –
> the taste of all things.

> Please, reveal Yourself and, my Beloved,
> Spread upon me the shelter of Your peace.
> Illuminate the world with Your glory.
> Let us rejoice and be happy in that.
> Hurry! Let in love, for that time has come.
> Show us grace for time eternal . . .

R. ELIEZER AZIKRI (16th century)

After evening services *Shabbat* is accepted into the home by the recitation of *kiddush* (Hebrew: sanctification) over a cup of wine. The table has been set in a festive manner. Candles have been lit in honour of the day. Some women light two candles, symbolizing the 'to keep' and the 'to remember' aspects of the holy day. Others light an additional candle for each of their children. You will also see on the table two braided loaves (*challot*) covered with a richly embroidered cloth. The loaves symbolize the double portions of manna which was received before *Shabbat*, during the forty years in the wilderness. The embroidered cover represents the dew which covered the manna. Symbol and suggestion abound. The very food which will be served is not without significance. Gefillte fish (Yiddish: 'filled' – that is ground and stuffed – fish), is prepared to avoid the prohibition of picking out the undesirable bones from the food. Cholent (a hot meat stew) recalls that, while it is forbidden to initiate cooking, it is permissible to keep it warm. This used to be a serious doctrinal issue between those who disputed the validity of the Oral Law.

The family members will go to synagogue in the morning to hear the weekly portions of the *Sefer Torah* being read. The whole five books of the Torah are read publicly during the course of a year. Each *Shabbat* morning the appropriate portion (*parsha*) is read, with seven people being called up to read it. Today, the reading is done by an expert, since the *Sefer Torah* is written without punctuation, vowels or cantillation marks. A relevant section from the Prophets (the *haftorah*) is also read.

The reading of the *Sefer Torah* is the central feature of the morning service, but the morning prayers have their own special richness. One of the most beautiful hymns was written by Rabbi Elazar Hakalir, who is said to have written it down after hearing it from the mouth of the Archangel Michael during a mystical vision:

. . . they prepared and fashioned the rays
   of the sun;
They made goodness to honour His name;
They placed the givers of light around
   His strength.
These leaders of the supernal, holy host are
   God' s praise.
Constantly they relate God' s glory and
   holiness . . .

With the appearance of the stars on Saturday
night, *Shabbat* is bid farewell with the *havdala*
ceremony (Hebrew: distinction), when blessings
are made on a cup of wine, fragrant spices or herbs,
and the light of a braided candle. The fragrance is
to revive the soul which yearns for continuous
Shabbat. The light from the braided candle recalls
that, while Adam and Chava (Eve) spent the first
Shabbat in the supernal light of the Garden, they
were sent out into darkness at the conclusion of the
day. The fire was the man-made attempt to create a
new light in the darkened world.

Havdala is often followed by a meal –
malava malka (Aramaic: escorting the Queen) –
whereas at the three meals of *shabbat* itself,
table songs are sung.

Keep in mind that the constraint/possibilities,
negative/positive equilibrium of *shabbat* is a model
for the other festivals. Similar laws apply to all

⊙ The havdala *ceremony marks the conclusion of* Shabbat. *The essential elements in this service are wine; sweet-smelling herbs or spices (often held in a silver tower-like container); and fire (provided by a braided candle)*

festivals, with the exception that limited food preparation is permitted on them.

The most frequent festival is that of *Rosh Chodesh*, the start of the lunar month. While technically a minor festival, it assumed such significance that the Syrian-Greek invaders

(200 BCE) forbade its celebration. Today, it is marked by additional morning prayers and slightly more festive food. Because of the monthly cycle of the festival, *Rosh Chodesh* has always been associated with women. As a result, it is a festival on which women try to meet for social or educational purposes on this day. Within the feminist movement, contemporary ritual and practice reflecting the cyclical nature of the festival have been developed.

Festivals Outside Israel

Outside Israel, festivals are generally observed for two days. Jewish chronology is based on a nineteen-year cycle, and incorporates both lunar and solar aspects to ensure that *Pesach* (Passover) always occurs in the spring. The exact times on which festivals fell were originally determined by a rabbinical court in the Temple, who used visual observation to fix the new lunar month. Today, these dates are determined mathematically and published in Jewish calendars. The very nature of the calendar means that festival dates vary from year to year.

During the time of the Temple, communication difficulties meant that communities outside Israel were never sure when any festival would occur and so, to be on the safe side, kept the festival for two days.

» The Jewish Year

Jewish months are determined by the moon and average 29.5 days (alternatively twenty-nine and thirty days). This would give a twelve-month year of 354 days, with the Jewish year receding eleven days every civil year. However, the festival of Pesach must fall in the spring and so an extra month (Adar II) is inserted into every second, or third, year.

All of this means that Jewish dates will fall on different dates on the civil calendar in different years. When scheduling events which will involve observant Jews, it is important to use a Jewish calendar (which is computed for the next two hundred years), or consult with someone who is knowledgeable about the Jewish calendar. The length of the festivals are given for the Diaspora; they are generally one day shorter in Israel.

MARCH/APRIL Pesach (Passover; Festival of Matzot; 'season of our freedom'). Festival of eight days, the first two and last two of which are like *Shabbat*.

MAY/JUNE Shavu'ot (Pentecost; Festival of the Harvest [wheat]; Festival of the First Fruits; 'season of being given our Torah'). Two-day festival like *Shabbat*, which occurs seven weeks (fifty days) after Pesach.

AUGUST Tisha b'Av (Ninth of the month of Av). Fast day for the destruction of the First and Second Temples.

SEPTEMBER/OCTOBER Rosh Hashana (New Year) Two-day festival like *Shabbat*.

SEPTEMBER/OCTOBER Yom Kippur (Day of Atonement; The Day of Judgement) One-day festival similar to *Shabbat* except that it is a day of fasting. Ten days after *Rosh Hashana*. These ten days are referred to as the Days of Awe.

SEPTEMBER/OCTOBER Sukkot (Tabernacles; Festival of the Booths; Festival of the Ingathering; 'the season of our joy'). Festival of seven days, the first two of which are like *Shabbat*. This festival is immediately followed by a two-day Sabbath-like festival, *Sh'mini At'tzeret* (The Convocation of the Eighth Day) and *Simchat Torah* (Rejoicing with the Law). In Israel this is a one-day festival.

DECEMBER Chanukka (Festival of Lights). Eight days of praise and thanksgiving with candles lit in evening.

FEBRUARY/MARCH Purim One day of feasting and rejoicing with the public reading of the *Book of Esther*.

⊙ Charging Philistine warriors with their characteristic plumed helmets; defeated
by the pharaoh Rameses III, they settled in Canaan and clashed with the
Israelites. From a twelfth-century BCE Egyptian stone relief

Since the lunar month averages twenty-nine-and-a-half days, the discrepancy between the 'official' month of Jerusalem and the month of the Diaspora never differed by more than that one – 'in-doubt' – day. Although communications are now instantaneous, and although festival dates are known in advance through calendar determinations, the custom maintained in the Diaspora is to observe major festivals on two consecutive days. In Israel, festivals are observed for one day, except for *Rosh Hashana* (New Year) when all communities observe two days.

'Pilgrimage' Festivals

There are three major festivals which are often called pilgrimage festivals. During the time of the Temple all those who could reasonably be expected to do so were expected to make the pilgrimage to Jerusalem and celebrate the festival there. Today, there is no requirement to celebrate these festivals in Jerusalem, and indeed they are celebrated in different Jewish communities around the world. These three great festivals are: *Pesach, Shavu'ot and Sukkot.*

Pesach (Passover)
This festival commemorates the Jewish exodus from Egypt. The festival lasts for seven days with a holy day (similar to *Shabbat*) at the beginning

and end of the period. Of special significance is the festive *seder,* which marks the first night (or first and second nights outside Israel). The extended family assembles to eat *matzot* (crisp wafers of unleavened bread) with bitter herbs (lettuce or horseradish); to drink four cups of wine, and to recite the *Hagadda* – a text which details the events surrounding the original exodus from Egypt.

Shavu'ot (Pentecost)
The second of these pilgrimage festivals, *Shavu'ot* is a festival which falls fifty (Greek: '*pente*') days after Pesach. *Shavu'ot* celebrates the receiving of the Torah at Mount Sinai. Many communities decorate their synagogues with green branches and plants because there is a tradition that at the time the Torah was received Mount Sinai was green and fragrant. On a culinary note, this festival – unlike all others – is celebrated with dairy meals: cheese cake, blintzes, etc. *Shavu'ot* is a single-day festival in Israel (two consecutive days elsewhere).

Sukkot
This concludes the three-pilgrimage festival cycle. It is an exceedingly joyful seven-day festival. Again, the first and last days being holy days, similar to *Shabbat.* This festival falls fifteen days after the Jewish New Year, *Rosh Hashana*, and five days after the Day of Atonement. Although it has

⊘ *Inner Sanctum of the Second Temple. Model in the Israel Museum, Jerusalem*

multiple significance, at its most obvious *Sukkot* alludes to the period immediately following the exodus, when Jewish people lived in temporary dwellings in the desert. Observant Jews build makeshift huts alongside their homes, thatching them with branches, reeds or bamboo. They will eat and sleep there during the seven days of the festival. In Hebrew the word *sukkot* means 'shelters', hence the Anglicized names for the festival: Tabernacles, or The Festival of Booths.

An interesting feature of *Sukkot* is the taking of the *arba minim* (the Four Species). This rather

⊙ Simchat Torah – *rejoicing with the Torah*

mystical rite involves shaking a bunch of four
distinct plants – a palm frond, myrtle and willow
branches, and a lemon-like fruit called an *etrog* – in
all six directions (east, west, north, south, up and
down). This is done during the morning prayers.
There is also a custom dating from the time of the
Prophets of beating a bunch of willow branches on
the ground.

The conclusion of *Sukkot* is immediately
followed by the very energetic, one-day festival of
Simchat Torah (Rejoicing of the Torah). Here the
rejoicing is for the possession – rather than for the
receiving – of the Torah. There is much dancing
and merriment. Customarily, the annual reading of
the *Sefer Torah* is concluded on this day.

Other Celebrations of the Jewish Year

Having examined the three major festivals, we can now look at some of the other celebrations in the Jewish year. There are different traditions, but if we choose to start the year with the already mentioned festival of *Pesach*, then the next minor festival is the thirty-third day of the Omer period, *Lag b'Omer*. (The Omer was a sheaf of the new barley harvest offered up in the Temple on the second day of Pesach). This is a festive break in what is normally a rather sombre fifty-day period, between *Pesach* and *Shavu'ot*. In Israel the custom is to light bonfires on that night and, if possible, to visit the tomb of the mystic Rabbi Shimon bar Yochai in Meron (Galilee), who died on this day some eighteen hundred years ago. The festival is also related to events in the life of Rabbi Akiva, who lived in the turbulent times which followed the destruction of the Second Temple by the Romans.

Some tragic events are also commemorated. *Tisha b'Av* (Hebrew: the ninth day of the month of Av) is a day of deep reflection commemorating the destruction of both First and Second Temples. It is a major fast day with many of the customs of formal mourning: no bathing, no wearing of leather shoes, etc. The Book of Lamentations is read in synagogues. Although a day of deep anguish, it is said that the Messiah will be born on that day.

Rosh Hashana

The month of Tishrai, which is the seventh month
after *Pesach*, is filled to the brim with festivals.
There is a tradition that all sevens are blessed.
The month of Tishrai begins with *Rosh Hashana*
(Hebrew: new year) which celebrates the creation
of Adam and Eve – humanity' s progenitors. *Rosh
Hashana* is celebrated in synagogue and at home.
In synagogue, a ram's horn (*shofar*) – an allusion to
the Binding of Isaac which took place on this day –
is blown a hundred times. At home the custom is to
eat bread and apples dipped in honey, symbolizing
the anticipation of a sweet year.

Rosh Hashana is called the day of judgement. On
it Jews, as individuals and as members of a nation,
are required to begin a period (known as 'the Days
of Awe') of repentance, which reaches its climax
ten days later with *Yom Kippur.* The symbolism
overshadowing this period is of God having opened
three great ledgers. Judgement on the indisputably
righteous and the unalterably wicked has been
recorded, however the vast majority of people are
provisionally listed in the third ledger – 'pending a
final decision'. The traditional blessing reflects this:
You should be written and sealed for the good.

How can the final decision be made positive?
The strident call of the *shofar* is a call to *t'shuva.*
the provisional judgement can always be

overturned by *t'shuva*. In Judaism *t'shuva* (literally 'return') does not simply mean remorse for past failings. Instead it encompasses two elements: (i) turning away from wrongdoing and approaching God and (ii) the commitment to refrain from transgression in the future.

During the Days of Awe there is the opportunity to become connected to Godliness. Penitential prayers are said. Efforts are made to observe more *mitzvot*. Donations are made to charities and good causes. In some communities fasts are undertaken. Following the afternoon service, congregants go to symbolically cast out their sin beside the sea, or rivers or similar bodies of water.

Just as the 'writing' was done on *Rosh Hashana*, so the 'sealing' is done on *Yom Kippur*. This is the day when the interim decree becomes finalized, at both an individual and national level.

Yom Kippur

Yom Kippur (Hebrew: the day of atonement) is on the tenth day of Tishrai. It is a festival day in spite of its inevitable solemnity. It is often called the Sabbath of Sabbaths. It is the custom to behave like the angels on this day: people dress in white and spend all day in synagogue; there is no eating, drinking or anointing with creams or oil; the wearing of leather shoes is prohibited, as are marital relations.

The prayers on this holy day ask for forgiveness at an individual, communal and even cosmic level. The word '*kippur*' means to avert an inevitable consequence: acts of charity, repentance and prayer can deflect the consequence of both individual and communal sin. While a powerful emotional atmosphere is built up in the extended prayers, the actual message is very simple. Thus, at the climax of the day, the *Cohen Ha'gadol* (the High Priest) would enter the Holy of Holies and request:

May it be Your will, God,
Our God, and the God of our fathers, that
    this year,
Which has come upon us and upon all of
    your people Israel
Where ever they may be,
Be a year of light;
A year of blessing;
A year of joy;
A year of pleasure;
A year of glory . . .

The afternoon service of *Yom Kippur* contains a Torah reading which enumerates, with stark clarity, the forbidden sexual relationships (incest, etc.). Any pretentions of ambiguity in the day evaporate: there are clearly delimited prohibitions and there are grave penalties for transgressions. In the time

of the Temple, determination of guilt and infliction
of punishment (which included death by stoning,
strangulation, decapitation or burning) were in the
hands of the High Court (the *Sanhedrin*) which sat
in Jerusalem. Today, no court has competency to
hear such cases: these issues are in the hands of
'the Heavenly Court' .

The service continues with the reading of the
Book of Jonah. The stark contrast between Jonah's
repeated failure to do God's bidding and the deep
level of repentance attained by the (non-Jewish)
people of Nineveh is poignant.

As the sun sinks, the *Ni'eela* (literally locking-
up) service begins. The gates of the Temple were
closed and locked at night. Likewise, the gates
of repentance are also about to be locked up
as night approaches. The emotional level of
the prayer reaches a climax. There is a
heightened sense of urgency among the
congregants who proclaim:

> Open for us the Gate, at this time of the
>   Gate's closing,
> For the day is fading.
> This day will fade away, the sun will set
>   and will fade.
> Let us come to the Gate.
> Please God – we implore You – please be stilled;
> Please forgive; please pardon; please have
>   compassion;

Please be merciful; please grant atonement;
please extinguish sin and iniquity.

The day of *Yom Kippur* ends with a single piercing blast of the *shofar*; there are simply no words left. The call of the *shofar* also links us back thematically to the festival of *Rosh Hashana* which we celebrated ten days before.

On the fifteenth day of Tishrai, five days after *Yom Kippur*, is the major festival of *Sukkot* which has been described above.

Chanukka

The festival of *Chanukka* (Hebrew: dedication) is often called the Festival of Light. It commemorates the revolt and victory of the Maccabees against the Syrian-Greeks (about 165 BCE). The Maccabees rededicated the defiled Temple and brought back pure light to the *menora*, the seven-branched candelabrum. Wax candles – or preferably lamps of olive oil – are lit every night in each home. The prevailing custom is to add one additional light each night through the eight-day period. These lights are lit in the windows so that they can be seen by passers-by. The ancient custom – and incidentally still the one which prevails in Jerusalem – is to light the lamps (sheltered in a glass case) outside the front door. *Chanukka* is 'a time of praise and thanksgiving'.

⊙ At Chanukka *flames are lit by the window to commemorate the victory of the Maccabees. During the eight-day festival an additional flame is lit every evening. The flames, from wax candles or olive oil, are lit in a* chanukkia, *which has eight side branches. The* menora *which stood in the Temple – and which is presently depicted on the seal of Israel – has seven branches*

Purim

Purim, by contrast, is 'a time of feasting and rejoicing'. It is a particularly joyous festival based on the events outlined in the Book of Esther. While of relatively minor religious significance, this festival is exceedingly popular. It is seen as emphasizing the 'hidden face of God' in world events. It also concludes the annual festival cycle. The Book of Esther is read in the evening and morning; children dress up in elaborate disguises and costumes; friends exchange gifts of food; gifts are distributed to the poor; and everybody is enjoined to feast and (especially) drink in deliberate excess!

⊙ A seventeenth-century European artist's 'grand' concept of Moses, walking next to the Ark of the Covenant, leading 600,000 Israelites through the wilderness

Chapter 5

Rituals & Customs

Ritual might convey a mechanical, external and vaguely symbolic act. That, however, would not do justice to what is about to be described. In Judaism, ritual is the enactment of a deeper underlying drama. Jewish ritual is always embedded in a rich matrix of Divine imperative, rabbinical reasoning or mystical allusion. Through the active performance in the ritual we are connected to this matrix.

Customs (*minhagim*) are the local product of Jewish communities. As might be expected customs, as opposed to rituals, show considerable diversity reflecting different cultural experiences in Jewish history. While it may be convenient, for example, to distinguish between the Ashkenazi Jews of Europe and the Sephardi Jews of the Mediterranean, these should be taken as a primary differentiation: there are considerable variations among each group. Further, Jewish customs found in the Yemen, Bukhara (Uzbekistan), Cochin (India) and Ethiopia seem remote and exotic to most Western Jews.

⊙ *Reading the Torah at* Bar Mitzvah

» Sephardi and Ashkenazi Jews

The Sephardi communities (Hebrew: Spain) came into being as a result of the forcible expulsion of the Jews from Spain in 1492. They settled the coast of North Africa, Bulgaria, Salonika, Venice and Turkey. Many of them still speak a smattering of old Spanish dialects mixed with Hebrew (Ladino). Many Ashkenazi Jews speak a *lingua franca* based on Old German with many Hebrew and local (e.g. Russian) language borrowings. This is called Yiddish.

Life-cycle Rituals

Let us look at the customs and commandments which occur in the Jewish life-cycle.

Circumcision

Eight days after birth, provided that he is in good health, the male baby is circumcised. This positive commandment recalls the covenant between God and the Patriarch Abraham. The circumcision (*brit mila*) is accompanied by celebration and festive meal. There is also a festive meal on the Friday night preceding the *brit*, or (in Sephardi communities) on the night immediately before, or on the third day following the circumcision.

Bar Mitzva

On the thirteenth birthday a boy is required to accept upon himself the 'yoke of the Kingdom of Heaven': he becomes a 'son of the *mitzvot*' – *bar mitzva*. This marks the age of legal majority in Jewish law. It is marked by the young man's first *aliya* (calling up to read the *Sefer Torah*) and with a festive meal.

Within the religious community the *bar mitzva* marks the beginning of a life dedicated to the precepts of the Torah and responsibility for one's spiritual actions. It is a joyful but serious affair. If, however, you attend a *bar mitzva* celebration in a

⊙ *Children studying one of the holy texts. Note that they both wear* kippot, *the head covering prescribed for males.* Kippot *(singular:* kippa*) come in all shapes, colours and sizes*

less committed Jewish setting you might see it – as do many of the Jewish participants – simply as an expensive party, or a cultural rite of passage. Regrettably, many a shortsighted thirteen-year-old sees his *bar mitzva* as the end – not the beginning – of things. He may have struggled with learning to recite his Torah portion, thinking that once the performance is done he can enjoy the food and accept the presents which will be lavished on him.

Bat Mitzva

Girls attain legal majority at the age of twelve. In many communities a parallel *bat mitzva* celebration has been instituted to give public expression to the young woman's coming of age. While such public celebrations are not common in Orthodox circles, private celebrations are becoming more common.

Marriage

Marriage is seen not simply as the union of two individuals but as the foundation of the continuation of a Jewish heritage. Both partners must be Jewish: marrying a non-Jew – marrying out – is viewed as both an individual and a national catastrophe.

The couple is married under a *chupa*, an embroidered canopy supported at each corner by a pole symbolizing the enveloping new home which the young couple are establishing within the Jewish nation.

The marriage is solemnized by the husband giving his bride a ring and a wedding contract (*ketuba*), which enumerates his obligations to her. These include providing for her financial support during the marriage and agreeing to pay alimony in the event of a divorce. The short service is tinged with remembrance of less pleasant things when a glass is shattered to recall the destruction of the Temple. Marriage is followed by seven days of festive meals at which blessings are bestowed on the couple.

Children/Education

Children are considered the most valuable product of a marriage, and perhaps of the whole community. The family is the central unit of normative Judaism. Education, as much as procreation, is required to preserve the continuum of the Jewish heritage. Continued learning of Jewish custom and law is an integral part of everyday Jewish life.

Bereavement and Mourning

Death, when it eventually comes, is always traumatic. The Jewish concept of grieving and mourning has two main components: strengthening the departing soul in its return to God, and consoling those who are left behind. The body of the deceased, which in rabbinical literature is referred to as 'a dented mirror' (since it once reflected the 'image of God'), is ritually washed and respectfully dressed in a shroud. Interment is completed as soon after death as possible.

The family is allowed to act out its sense of profound loss. It is considered that expression of grief is therapeutic and the family will sit for seven days (*shiva*) remembering the departed with friends and acquaintances who will call. There are many customs associated with dying, death and bereavement, but none obscures the basic concept of giving comfort and strength to the dying and those they leave behind.

If you are invited to a Jewish house of mourning you might find it helpful to keep the following points in mind:

- the last days of the *shiva* are generally less harrowing than the first
- do not bring gifts or flowers with you
- sit only when the bereaved are seated
- do not make conversation; let the bereaved speak first
- expect those present to talk about the deceased
- allow the bereaved to show emotion
- allow the bereaved to talk openly about their loss
- when you leave you will not be expected to use the formal Hebrew formula which is used on these occasions; however, do approach the bereaved and extend your condolences.

Annual Remembrance

Yahrzeit (Yiddish: a year's time), is the annual remembrance of the dead of a close relative. The event is marked in different ways, depending on local custom, but a common theme is the lighting of a memorial candle on the night of the anniversary and the saying of *kaddish*. Charity donations are commonly made to mark such events. It is understood that a deed of compassion done in the name of the deceased will further elevate his/her soul.

Divorce and Family Law

While it is not, hopefully, an inevitable part of the life-cycle, perhaps we should also consider the concept of divorce. Either party may initiate the proceedings; the husband by directly divorcing his wife, she by going before a rabbinic court (*bet din*) and asking that the divorce be granted. If the rabbinic courts agree, the husband may be coerced into giving his permission to grant the bill of divorce (called a *get*).

In Israel, where the rabbinic courts have jurisdiction in most matters of family law, considerable legal pressure may be brought to bear on the erring husband. Once a divorce has been granted the husband is required, under the conditions set out in the wife' s wedding contract, to pay alimony.

Marriage is permissible to the divorced partners with only limited restrictions. Permanent separations should be finalized by the issuance of a bill of divorce, which allows both partners to remarry. If the ex-partners fail to obtain a *get* but subsequently marry these unions may be deemed adulterous. In terms of Jewish law, the children of adulterous or incestuous unions are legally stigmatized. Couples should always seek competent rabbinic advice before marriage, especially if there has been a previous marriage.

Daily Rituals

Daily life in Jewish society is punctuated by many rituals, while a rich tradition of art has often been associated with the desire to beautify these rituals.

⊙ T' fillin *are leather boxes containing passages from the Torah. They are positioned on head and upper forearm, and held in place by leather straps. They are worn at morning prayers by males over the age of thirteen*

Covering The Head: The *Kippa*

The custom among observant men is to cover the head at all times with a *kippa*. This is done out of reverence for God. Observant women also cover their heads (with a kerchief, or with a wig) for reasons of piety and modesty. In the Diaspora it has become common for men only to cover their heads while at prayer, although many younger men have taken to wearing the *kippa* out of an identification with Jewish tradition, if not out of piety. Whether the head is covered by a crocheted *kippa*, or a black beaver hat, or a richly embroidered Bukharian cap, or a turban, depends on the local culture: it is not a religious issue.

Morning Prayer: The *T'fillin*

During morning prayer men wear *t'fillin*. These are black, square leather boxes attached by leather straps to the head and the upper part of the arm. *T'fillin* contain parchment strips with the four Torah portions which detail this *mitzva*. *T'fillin* are an example of an *ot* (Hebrew: sign), an external remembrance of commandments, and are the subject of much esoteric literature in Jewish circles. Incidentally, the word 'phylacteries' (Greek: amulets) is an interesting example of an intercultural misreading: *t'fillin* are not magical charms.

The *Tallit* and *Tzitzit*

At morning prayer the male will also wear a *tallit*, a prayer shawl. This is done in order to fulfil yet another Torah injunction, which requires *tzitzit* to be made on the corners of all four-cornered garments. *Tzitzit* are fine woolen cords which are doubled and knotted onto each corner of the garment. Today, four-corner garments are somewhat out of style and so the *tallit* is specifically manufactured to fulfil the precept. Many people wear a smaller version of this garment during the day (normally under their shirt). Among the Ultra-Orthodox you may see this garment worn on top of the shirt.

It is perhaps worth pointing out that apart from *tzitzit* no particular religious significance is attached to other clothing. Jews from London may wear sports jackets or three-piece suits; the Chassidic Jews from Williamsburg (New York) may wear long coats and hard black hats (reminiscent of nineteenth-century Hungary or Romania); the older Jews from the Yemen may sport turbans and flowing robes; women from the Jewish communities of India may wear the sari. These are all interesting cultural artifacts rather than religious prerequisites. Judaism is pragmatic about external cultural adaptation and Jews have freely borrowed from (and often zealously retained) features of the non-Jewish world which surrounds them.

Mezuza: The Doorpost Scroll

The Torah also requires that Jewish doorways have a *mezuza* attached to the doorpost. A *mezuza* (Hebrew: doorpost) is a small parchment scroll on which has been written the first two sections of the *Sh'ma Yisrael* prayer where this *mitzva* is mentioned. The *mezuza* is enclosed in a decorative case and fixed to the upper third of the doorpost. If you visit Israel you will see a *mezuza* on all doorways of public and private buildings, including banks, hospitals, etc. Since the *mezuza* must be meticulously hand-written you will also find a large number of scribes at work.

⌃ The mezuza *scroll is fixed to the doorposts of Jewish dwellings*

Hand-washing

Before eating bread the hands are ritually washed. This is to remember the degree of purity which was required by those eating food within the precincts of the Temple. When the Temple was destroyed the rabbis decided to institute the washing of hands even for normal meals where bread was eaten.

Food and Drink Blessings

Blessings before and after eating and drinking were also instituted by rabbinic decree. Such blessings affirm that the individual has a right to satisfy him/herself with God's creation, but only after acknowledging the supremacy of God.

Kashrut: Food Laws

Kashrut (Hebrew: fit, in the sense of appropriate) encompasses a considerable set of laws dealing with whether a particular food can be eaten. For instance, meat can only be eaten if (i) it came from an animal which was permissible (such as cattle, sheep, chickens, turkey, etc.); (ii) the animal was killed according to the laws of *sh'chita* (the arteries are cleanly severed with a razor-sharp knife); (iii) the subsequent examination revealed that the carcass was free of

» Is it 'Kosher' ?

These laws obviously have social and spiritual dimensions: they restrict eating out with non-Jews; they sensitize those who keep *kasher* to what they eat. You may be familiar with the word 'kosher', which is the Ashkenazi (European) pronunciation of the (Hebrew) word *kasher*. In many States in America, local laws ensure that things described as 'kosher' are indeed in conformity with Jewish law.

damage and certain pathological conditions; (iv) the meat was properly treated with salt to extract blood; and (v) the resulting meat was cooked in a permissible manner. Cooking meat with milk, for instance, would render both not *kasher.*

Kashrut may seem somewhat esoteric, but it is a fundamental practice in everyday life for many Jews. Perhaps a few statistics from the largest market for *kasher* products – America – might be helpful. In 1994 this market segment bought non-meat products totaling $33,000 million. It is a fast-growing, upmarket sector, which many non-Jewish food manufactures are eager to enter. To do so they must arrange for rabbinic inspection of their products. The non-meat market sector includes not only the estimated 800,000 American families who eat only *kasher* products, but also four million Moslems and about six million vegetarians who rely on rabbinical certification that these products are meat free.

Chapter 6

Holy Texts

Jews have a deep and abiding relationship with their holy texts. Jewish tradition teaches that the letters of the Hebrew alphabet, and writing itself, were mystical elements in Creation. Holy books have in themselves the attribute of holiness. When books are stacked one on top of the other they are arranged according to their degree of holiness, the holiest on top. We learn that when Moses received the Ten Commandments they were written by the 'finger of God' on a sapphire cube.

An integral part of being a knowledgeable Jew is the ability to read and comprehend Jewish texts. The compliment paid to a competent scholar is: He knows how to learn for himself. It is axiomatic within Judaism that all have access to the same texts. There is no sacrosanct interpreter or keeper of knowledge.

The *Tanach*

Of central importance is the *chumash*. This is the printed text of the *Sefer Torah*. It is the same text which Moses copied in letters of fire on Mount

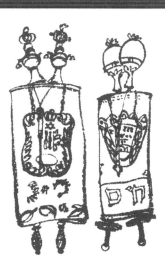

Richly decorated covers protect the scrolls of the Torah ⊙

Sinai. It is also known as the Written (contrasted with the Oral) Law.

If you examine a copy of the *chumash*, you will see that the sacred text occupies the centre of the page, with a translation in Aramaic written beside it. This translation (*targum*) was completed by Onkelos, a convert to Judaism in the time of the Romans. On the outside margins of the page you will see commentaries which discuss words, sentences and concepts in the

text. On almost all printed versions you will
see the commentary of Rashi, the acronym
of Rabbi Shlomo ben Itzchak (1040–1105),
whose work is still considered the most succinct
and informative.

There are literally hundreds of commentaries on
the *chumash*, each one exploring a certain theme or
avenue. Some will concentrate on clarifying the
words and phrases used; others will look for ethical
messages; yet others may explore numerical
relationships (*gematria*), since Hebrew letters also
have numerical equivalents.

While the Torah has a unique history of
revelation, it is not the only revealed text in
Judaism. The books of the Prophets (*Nevi'im*),
which contain their visions, are also considered
to have been directly communicated. These
testimonies by people such as Isaiah, Ezekiel,
Ezra and Nechamia, attest to God's continuing
desire to direct and shape the history of the
Jewish nation.

There is a third set of texts, called *Ketuvim*
(Hebrew: writings), which record the words and
wisdom of David and Solomon (Psalms, Proverbs,
etc.) and include books such as those of Ruth and
of Esther. The latter marks the last text to be
included in the accepted Jewish canon.
Collectively, these three sets of holy texts –
Torah, Nevi'im and *Ketuvim* – are known by their
acronym: the *Tanach*.

» The Books of the *Tanach*

If you are familiar with the Bible, then you are already familiar with the core of Jewish revealed texts. You should be sensitive to the fact that for the Jew there is no 'new' or 'old' when referring to God's testaments. Similarly 'Jewish Bible' is a term which is best avoided; *'Tanach'* is the more culturally attuned. The Hebrew names of the books of the *Tanach* are shown with their English equivalents in parentheses.

TORAH

B'raishit (Genesis); *Sh'mot* (Exodus); *Va'yikra* (Leviticus); *Bamidbar* (Numbers); *D'varim* (Deuteronomy).

NEVI'IM

Yehoshua (Joshua); *Shoftim* (Judges); *Sh'muel* (Samuel); *Melachim* (Kings); *Yishiyahu* (Isaiah); *Yirmiyahu* (Jeremiah); *Yechezkel* (Ezekiel); *Hosai'a* (Hosea); *Yoel* (Joel); *Amos* (Amos); *Ovadia* (Obadiah); *Yona* (Jonah); *Mica* (Micah); *Nachum* (Nahum); *Chabakkuk* (Habakkuk); *Tzafania* (Zephaniah); *Chagay* (Haggai); *Zecharia* (Zechariah); *Malachi* (Malachi).

KETUVIM

T'hillim (Psalms); *Mishlai* (Proverbs); *Iyyov* (Job); *Shir Ha'shirim* (Song of Songs); *Rut* (Ruth); *Eicha* (Lamentations); *Kohelet* (Ecclesiastes); *Esther* (Esther); *Daniel* (Daniel); *Ezra-Nechemia* (Ezra, Nehemiah); *Divrai Hayamim* (Chronicles).

⊙ *Section of a third-century CE frieze found in the ruins of a synagogue near the Sea of Galilee showing an early mobile representation of the Ark of the Covenant*

The *Mishna* and Talmud

The Oral Law is understood to have begun with the experience at Mount Sinai and to have continued on, as a received tradition, until the compilation of the *Mishna*. In the centuries which followed the destruction of the Second Temple, the Jewish scholars of both Israel and Babylon continued to keep an oral tradition of Jewish law and wisdom. There was some resistance to reducing this tradition to writing, but under the direction of Yehuda Hanasi (towards the end of the second century CE), the oral tradition was collected, edited and recorded in the *Mishna*. The *Mishna* consists of six sections (or 'orders'), dealing with: (i) agricultural laws; (ii) the *shabbat* and the festivals; (iii) laws related to women; (iv) civil damages; (v) the Temple and the sacrifices which took place there; (vi) laws of defilement and ritual purity.

These Mishnaic texts formed the core of the study and debate in the rabbinical colleges of the period. A summation of the received opinions was compiled by the end of the sixth century. The Babylonian Talmud is an encyclopaedic work dealing not only with legal arguments, prevalent custom, and social observation but with almost every conceivable subject. It is published in twenty volumes (available on CD ROM, if you prefer) and can take a lifetime to study.

The Babylonian Talmud seems to reflect the society in which it came into being. There is a concern for the legal aspects of commerce and property. The Palestinian Talmud, by contrast, is a considerably smaller compilation from the Jewish academies of Israel. Here the concentration is more on agricultural laws, which were still a very real part of the life of the people in Israel.

❯❯ The Talmud – Core Source of Jewish Learning

The Talmud is the core source of Jewish learning, yet it is a difficult work to master. Firstly, it was written in Aramaic and not Hebrew. Secondly, its style is sparse and staccato-like, with a system of reasoning which is elegant and austere. Thirdly, it mirrors the debates which it records – tangents keenly pursued. Fourthly, it records the reasoning and arguments but not necessarily the final and accepted outcome of a legal debate. All of these factors led to many attempts to codify this massive body of learning.

The Codes of Jewish Law

There are many guides and compilations of the primary sources of Jewish tradition. The *Mishneh Torah* of the Rambam was completed in 1168 and is characterized by its clear, systematic ordering of the Talmud, interwoven with rich discussions on philosophy and the natural sciences (as we have seen, the Rambam was a practising physician). The *Mishneh Torah* has endured time and criticism, and is widely studied today. It is perhaps the finest and most comprehensive attempt to systematize the corpus of Jewish knowledge.

Josef Karo (1488–1575) compiled a massive and exceedingly influential work called the *Shulchan Aruch* (Hebrew: Prepared Table) in which he meticulously delineated the framework of law which surrounds the Jew. This work, which has been extensively augmented, footnoted and expanded remains the central text upon which Jewish legal decisions are based.

The *Shulchan Aruch* was extremely popular and soon scholars added to it and sought to augment its clear-cut lines. Today, a printed page of this work resembles an intricate patchwork of opinions, comments and references surrounding one or two lines of the original text. This in turn led to a number of attempts to produce an integrated, linear text more suitable for the reader who lacks the skill to balance all of the competing points of view.

There has also been a trend to simplify and shorten the legal codes, making them more accessible to the non-scholar. Similarly, there has been a considerable market interest in contemporary translations and compilations of all Jewish texts. The English reader has never before had such an opportunity to access Jewish learning.

While the above-mentioned texts are important, they cannot be regarded simply as books which line the shelves of a library. An intimate aspect of these holy texts is the ongoing study of them by Jewish men and women of every walk of life. While great respect is rightly accorded to a *talmid chacham* (a competent scholar) there is no preconception that scholarship is restricted to designated individuals or groups. The *Mishna* itself teaches that the question is not whether we have assimilated all of this knowledge, but rather whether we have begun.

A Sea of Knowledge

The amassed volume of Jewish knowledge is daunting: it is likened to a great sea. It has always been the custom, among scholars at least, to review large amounts of this material on a daily basis. For example, there are those who review eighteen chapters of the *Mishna* every day after morning prayers. At this rate the entire *Mishna* is completed on a monthly cycle. (Less adept scholars often settle for a chapter-and-a-half daily, completing the work in a year.) A daily review of Torah is both necessary and stimulating. The Rambam suggests that every Jew sets aside time to study every day, dividing that time equally between the study of *Tanach, Mishna* and the Talmud.

In recent times, there has been a trend to set up study groups which allow individuals, even with a very modest understanding of Hebrew, to systematically work through this treasury of Jewish thought. *Shabbat* study groups that discuss the weekly Torah reading are widespread, as are daily meetings to study a single page of the *Talmud*. Recently, there has been a keen interest, among religious circles, in learning a chapter of the Rambam daily (completing his monumental work in three years).

A familiarity with this literature of holiness is imperative for the contemporary Jew. Although a dynamic and accommodating religion, Judaism has a centre of gravity which lies beyond time and place. The literature of holiness, in which the Jew is immersed, is neither dated nor only a product of its time: it is a gateway to a relationship with an eternal God.

Chapter 7

Prayer & Liturgy

Public and Private

Prayer within Judaism has both a public and a private role. Prayer is public in two senses: it is offered within a public setting (usually the synagogue), and it addresses issues of public (communal/national) welfare. Its origins parallel the public sacrifices which were conducted during the time of the Temple. Today, when the Temple still lies in ruins, public prayer has taken over the function of sacrifice.

When Temple rites were practised all Jews were required to donate the same small amount of money (half a shekel) which was deposited in the treasury of the Temple. Three times a year this money was disbursed and sacrificial animals bought with it. Every day, sacrifices were made in the morning and late afternoon, on behalf of the collective Jewish nation. On *shabbat* and festival days additional sacrifices were made and today these offerings are also reflected in public prayer.

Private prayer is considered to be a matter quite separate from formal community prayer. Within

Wearing t'fillin *at morning prayer*

Jewish tradition, individuals are encouraged to approach God at any time, in any place, with any request. Private prayer is an intimate coming together of the supplicant and his/her Creator. Even in the main body of worship which constitutes public prayer, there are places for personal meditation, introspection and requests.

All prayer is a process of communication. While private prayer has indisputably a personal – not to say uniquely intimate – dimension, it would be wrong to consider public prayer either mechanical or distanced. Indeed, within many communities fervour in prayer is considered the hallmark of a refined, religious Jew. The expression of this fervour may differ markedly in different communities: chassidim may move backwards and forwards as they pray; others may call out; yet others may *davven* (Yiddish: to pray) at great length and with minimal movement.

Public Prayers: *Shacharit* – the Morning Service

Jewish males are required to pray three times a day. The morning prayer (*shacharit*) and the afternoon prayer (*mincha*) have replaced the daily sacrifices, although there is evidence that even during Temple times these prayers were said. The evening prayer (*ma'ariv*) was a rabbinical addition although it, too, alludes to Temple service.

The regular weekday *shacharit* is the longest of the three daily prayers. Ideally it should be prayed in synagogue, with a *minyan* (that is, a quorum of ten adult males), and dressed in *tallit* and *t'fillin*. The service is led by a *ba'al t'filla* (Hebrew: a master of prayer) who should be familiar with the prayers and the laws relating to them. He need not, however, be a rabbi or a person of impressive piety. Those in the first year of mourning for a close relative (parent, wife, etc.) are encouraged to lead at least part of the service if they are able.

The morning service is divided into a number of quite well defined sections. In most rites prayer opens with the beautiful anthem *Adon Olam* (Hebrew: Master of the Universe) written by Rabbi Shlomo ibn Gabriol (1021–69):

> Master of the Universe:
> You reigned before any form was created.
> Then, from the time that all things were brought
> into being,
> You desired that we know You as King.
> After everything will no longer be in existence,
> You will rule in unfathomable unity.
> He was. He is. He will be in supernal beauty.
> He is One: Nothing can be substituted for Him,
> Or compared to Him, or equated with Him . . .

The service continues with a series of blessings; Torah and Mishnaic passages related to *korbanot*; a series of Psalms and the song which Moses sang at the crossing of the Red Sea. The basic fabric of the liturgy comprises a wealth of biblical passages, particularly the Prophets and the Book of Psalms. For instance, the last set of Psalms are included in this part of the service.

Hallelu-ya. Give praise to God in all places.
Praise His power in the skies.
Praise Him for His might.
Praise Him as His greatness requires.
Praise Him with the shofar.
Praise Him with stringed instruments.
Praise Him with drum and dance.
Praise Him with wind instruments.
Praise him with clear and strident cymbals.
Let all that have a soul praise God. Hallelu-ya.
Let all that have a soul praise God. Hallelu-ya.

Psalm 150

The initial service is concluded with the recital of *kaddish* (see page 112) The major section now opens with *Baruch Hu* (Let us bless God, who should be blessed) and includes the blessing which surrounds the profoundly simple statement of faith, the *Sh'ma Yisrael*:

Hear O Israel, the Lord is our God, the Lord
   is one.
And you shall love God your God with all
your heart, and with all your soul, and with
all your strength. And these words, which I
shall command you this day, shall be upon
your hearts. And you shall instruct your
children in them, and shall speak of them
when you sit in your house, when you walk
in the way, when you lie down and when

you rise up. And you shall tie them as a sign
on your arm and have them as a commendation
between your eyes. And you shall write them
on the doorposts of your houses and your gates.

Deuteronomy 6:4–9

The *Sh'ma Yisrael* is followed by the *amida*
(Hebrew: standing), a silent prayer recited while
standing. The prayer contains nineteen blessings
ending in one for *shalom*. Incidentally, the Hebrew
word for peace (*shalom*) means a unified complete-
ness rather than simply the absence of dissension.
When the *amida* has been completed by individual
members of the congregation it is repeated by the
ba'al t'filla. During this repetition the congregation
respond to the *kedusha* (the declaration of God's
holiness), standing erect, feet together, like the
angels of Isaiah's vision (*Isaiah 6:3*):

Holy, Holy, Lord of hosts,
The whole earth is filled with your honour.

The repetition of the *amida* is normally followed
by prayers of confession and repentance, unless
the day is a festival. Additional passages are
inserted in the *amida* if the day is a minor festival
(*Rosh Chodesh*, the intermediate day of *Sukkot*, or
Pesach, etc.). On Mondays, Thursdays and festival
days the *Sefer Torah* is read although the section
selected is appreciably shorter than on *Shabbat*.

The morning service is then concluded with more Psalms and passages from the *Mishna*.

The prayers on *Shabbat* and festivals are very similar to the above except that the *amida* has only seven blessings. *Shabbat* services are more relaxed and the prayers will be led with much singing and ornamentation on the part of the *ba'al t'filla*. *Shabbat* and festival services also include an Additional Service (*musaf*) reflecting the additional set of sacrifices brought on such days in the Temple.

The service is punctuated at various points by the recitation of the *kaddish*, a short prayer in Aramaic which magnifies and exalts the name of God. Aramaic was the lingua franca of Jews following the Babylonian exile (586–38 BCE). This language, the language of the Babylonian Talmud, has found its way into prayer books in a limited way. There are a number of variants of *kaddish* marking different sections in the service. *Kaddish* may only be recited if there is a *minyan* present.

Women are exempted from public prayer, although many take that obligation upon themselves. Women are considered, in a very profound and mystical sense, to be beyond the dimension of time. In general, they are not required to observe positive commandments which are time-bound, such as, for example, public prayer. It should be noted that while women are generally exempted from positive commandments, they are bound to observe prohibitions irrespective of whether time is an element.

Public Prayers: The Afternoon and Evening Services

The afternoon service (*mincha*) is, in contrast to the morning service, very short. In essence it consists of the *amida* which is prayed silently by the congregation and then repeated by the *ba'al t'filla*. *Kedusha* and *kaddish* are also said.

The evening service (*ma'ariv or aravit*) is likewise short. It consists of the *Sh'ma Yisrael* with the blessings which come before and after it. These are followed by a recitation of the *amida*. However, this prayer is not repeated by the *ba'al t'filla*.

Liturgy: The Order of Prayer

The order of prayer, and many of the major prayers themselves, were instituted by the Elders of the Great Assembly about the third century BCE. While there is considerable community variation in the detail, the structure of the services is remarkably uniform. Most large communities have produced their own prayer book or *siddur* (Hebrew: an ordering) which embody their unique experiences and history. Prayer books tend to follow a rule of accretion: new prayers are reluctantly added, old ones even more reluctantly abandoned. The major division is between the Ashkenazi (European) and Sephardi (Mediterranean) rites but the distinction is largely one of section order and word detail.

Festival prayers, particularly for *Rosh Hashana* and *Yom Kippur*, are extended. They contain many poems and meditations, particularly from the medieval period, and are a rich source of inspiration, history and archaic usage of Hebrew. As one might expect, it is within these prayer books that the greatest degree of community variation can be found.

Within the Jewish Orthodox world public prayer is always conducted in Hebrew. Hebrew was created as an explicit holy language. It is the universal medium of prayer and prayers said in that language are effective even if the person is not totally familiar with the language. For private prayer any language is effective. When praying in Hebrew at least some understanding of the simple meaning of the words is preferable.

» Praying in Hebrew

The fact that prayer is conducted in Hebrew means that Jewish children must acquire a proficiency in at least reading that language. Fortunately, modern Hebrew is still not too far removed from the classical, or biblical, language; indeed, although modern Hebrew has been quick to accumulate slang and idiomatic usage, the similarity between it and biblical Hebrew is considerably closer than between modern and Shakespearian English.

ברכת המזון

בָּרוּךְ אַתָּה יְיָ אֱלֹהֵינוּ מֶלֶךְ הָעוֹלָם· הַזָּן
אֶת־הָעוֹלָם כֻּלּוֹ· בְּטוּבוֹ בְּחֵן בְּחֶסֶד וּבְרַחֲמִים·
הוּא נוֹתֵן לֶחֶם לְכָל־בָּשָׂר· כִּי לְעוֹלָם חַסְדּוֹ:
וּבְטוּבוֹ הַגָּדוֹל תָּמִיד לֹא־חָסַר לָנוּ וְאַל יֶחְסַר־
לָנוּ מָזוֹן לְעוֹלָם וָעֶד בַּעֲבוּר שְׁמוֹ הַגָּדוֹל· כִּי
הוּא זָן וּמְפַרְנֵס לַכֹּל וּמֵטִיב לַכֹּל וּמֵכִין מָזוֹן
לְכָל־בְּרִיּוֹתָיו אֲשֶׁר בָּרָא· בָּרוּךְ אַתָּה יְיָ· הַזָּן
אֶת־הַכֹּל:

⌄ Grace after meals

Chapter 8

Of *Cohanim*, Levites & Rabbis

Within contemporary Judaism there exists no religious class system. The whole Jewish nation was selected by God to be a separate people dedicated to God – a nation of priests. At an individual level, the potential exists for each and every Jew to develop a unique and holy relationship with God. At a national level, the entire, united Jewish nation is also challenged to fulfil God's mission. No genetic, or social, advantage exists which favours the spiritual development of any particular group within this 'chosen nation'.

While Jews have a great appreciation of lineage, and while positive attention will certainly be given to someone who comes from a prestigious family, the only way of acquiring 'status' in the Jewish religious world is through Jewish scholarship and/or a life devoted to fulfilment of the *mitzvot*. This has been particularly evident in recent generations, where the *ba'al t'shuva* – the non-religious person who returns to Jewish observance – has been seen as a potent exemplar of the Jewish mission.

⊗ *Blowing the ram's horn at* Rosh Hashana *(New Year)*

In spite of this egalitarian approach, there are some well recognized divisions and levels within Judaism, for instance the *cohanim*, the Levites and the rabbis.

Cohanim

Within Judaism there is a priestly caste (the *cohanim*) which traces its lineage back to the original High Priest, Aaron, older brother of Moses.

Aaron was entrusted to bring sacrifices within the *mishkan* in the period of wandering in the desert. His male descendants – priesthood is transmitted via the patrimonial line – continued to perform Temple service when the Jewish people entered the land of Israel.

During the times of the First and Second Temple, the *cohanim* constituted a sizeable and influential proportion of the people. They were organized in twenty-four regional districts and took turns in going up to Jerusalem to participate in the Temple services. A core of full-time *cohanim*, under the direction of the High Priest (*Cohen Ha'gadol*), instructed and supervised these volunteers.

The primary function of the *cohanim* was to conduct the services in the Temple. They had exclusive right to enter the inner courtyard of the sanctuary. The *Cohen Ha'gadol* alone was permitted to enter the deepest parts of the Temple (the Holy of Holies) and did so only for a brief period on Yom Kippur. Indeed, during that day he performed all the major parts in the ritual of seeking atonement from God for all the Jewish people.

The *cohanim* were not priests in the sense of intermediaries. They facilitated the sacrifices – either on behalf of individuals or on behalf of the entire Jewish nation (the daily public sacrifices) – but were not indispensable. They are seen as having an intrinsic degree of *kedusha*, which is usually translated as holiness. In Hebrew *kedusha* means 'dedicated for a special purpose'. This degree of *kedusha* means that males are restricted in terms of whom they can marry (no divorcees, for example) and the forms of defilement which they must avoid (contact with the dead).

With the destruction of the Second Temple, much of the functional duties of the *cohanim* were suspended. However, they still perform privileged functions and receive considerable respect. Thus they receive the first *aliya* (the first to read) when the *Sefer Torah* is read; lead the grace after meals; bless the congregation (on Festivals or, as in Israel, daily); and redeem the first-born child.

Levites

While Aaron was chosen to be the High Priest it was his clan (the Levites) who earned the honour of guarding and transporting the *mishkan*. They also assisted the *cohanim* in their sacrificial duties. Levites were also entitled to tithes from agricultural products grown by the remaining Israelite tribes.

When the Temple was established in Jerusalem, the Levites acted as guards. They were also accomplished musicians and singers and accompanied many of the Temple services. Again, as with the *cohanim*, their special role within Jewish society was suspended when the Temple was destroyed.

Today, vestigial traces of their special honour exist, for example, they are given the second *aliya* (second to read) when the *Sefer Torah* is read.

Rabbis

Rabbis acquire their title through study and subsequent ordination by an existing rabbi or rabbinical court. The candidate must be of good character and be conversant with the extensive body of laws relating to everyday Jewish life. In Israel, the Chief Rabbinate offers public examinations for any suitably qualified candidate.

The rabbi is, in essence, an expert in Jewish law. He will be consulted and asked to give a legal decision on issues which can range from whether a cooking pot is still kosher to whether life-support systems on a brain-dead patient can be removed. He is not a priest, in the sense of being a spiritual intermediary in Jewish religious life.

A rabbi may take a further qualification in order to be able to decide on cases dealing with more complex or monetary matters. Thus qualified the *Dayan* (Hebrew: judge) will sit on a rabbinical court (*bet din*), usually with another two colleagues. All large communities have a *bet din* hearing cases involving family and civil law (divorce, contractual disputes, etc.).

Within the Orthodox world only males have obtained rabbinic ordination. In many of the other contemporary expressions of Judaism (Reform, Liberal, etc.), where the role of the rabbi is perceived as predominantly one of pastoral caring, women also serve as rabbis.

» The Rabbi's Skills

Rabbi Shimshon Rafael Hirsch explains that the word 'rabbi' is derived from a Hebrew root meaninq 'to duplicate', because his example should be worthy of emulation. The present-day rabbi will be consulted on sensitive personal issues such as family counselling, where his sensitivity and communication skills will be valued. While originally looked upon as a legal authority, there is an increasing demand for rabbis to develop superior communication and interpersonal skills.

Chapter 9

Pilgrimages & Places Of Worship

Pilgrimages are not simply physical journeys: they are journeys towards a spiritual goal. In its purely physical sense, pilgrimage is no longer an essential part of Jewish practice, although there are those who would say that the Jew is on a continual pilgrimage in this world. In the time of the Temple, pilgrimage to Jerusalem for the three major festivals was incumbent on those living reasonably close to the city.

Places are nevertheless considered to be imbued with significance, meaning and holiness. Visiting the graves of the righteous is an ancient custom. In Israel even marginally religious people will visit such tombs in Jerusalem and also in the holy cities of:

- Hebron (also known as Kiriat Arba), where the Patriarchs and Matriarchs are interred (with the exception of Rachel who lies in a tomb just outside Bethlehem)
- Meron, where Rabbi Shimon bar Yochai is buried
- Safed, where many of the sixteenth-century Kabbalists are buried, including the Ari' zal (Rabbi Yitzchak Luria, 1534–72)
- Tiberius, where the Rambam is buried

⊙ *Praying at the Western or "Wailing" Wall – the surviving outer wall of the
Second Temple in Jerusalem*

In Israel, Europe and even America, Chassidim will go to the graves of their *rebbes* (spiritual leaders). Visitors at such sites will offer prayers (particularly in the form of Psalms), give to charity and light candles. Among the Sephardim there is a beautiful custom of making a blessing over fragrant herbs at such sites.

The Land of Israel

There is no positive commandment to visit Israel, but many make the journey nonetheless. The Land of Israel is understood to have a level of holiness which, according to most authorities, still exists. This holiness is reflected in the special treatment of crops grown there (the taking of tithes) and in the restriction on the land in every seventh (*sh'mita*) year. In Temple times the conclusion of the seventh *sh'mita* cycle, that is every fiftieth year, was marked as a *yovel*, hence the English word 'jubilee'.

It is considered meritorious for a Jew to be buried in Israel and many who live in the Diaspora are in fact interred there. Even for those buried outside Israel it is the custom to sprinkle them – immediately prior to burial – with soil brought over from the Holy Land.

Jerusalem

The city of Jerusalem has an even higher level of holiness and the remnants of the Temple – the

Western Wall and the Temple Mount – a still higher level. The Wall is visited by many thousands of people every day – secular and religious. The Wall is the remaining section of the external wall which surrounded the Temple Mount. It is the custom to leave a note, bearing a request or even simply one's name, in the crevices between the stones. The Wall can be visited by Jews or non-Jews.

» Choosing Direction for Prayer

When praying it is desirable for those in the Diaspora to face east (that is in the general direction of Israel); for those in Israel to face Jerusalem; for those in Jerusalem to face in the direction of the site of the Temple, and for those beside the site of the Temple to face towards the Holy of Holies.

The Synagogue

Religious services can take place anywhere: a special building and a special setting is not required. If, however, a community is established there is a duty upon them to erect, or dedicate, a special place for communal worship or study. The synagogue (Greek: house of assembly) is specially built for these purposes. The traditional synagogue mirrors the main features of the *mishkan*, which was eventually established as the First and Second Temples in Jerusalem.

⌃ *Ark of the Great Synagogue in Dohány Street, Budapest*

In a modern synagogue, the eastern wall houses
the ark where the scrolls of the *Sefer Torah* are
housed. The ark may contain many scrolls, donated
to the synagogue by individuals to commemorate
special events. The ark is often elaborately
decorated and screened by an ornate curtain
(*parochet*). Within the Ashkenazi tradition, the

Sefer Torah is attached to a pair of wooden rollers, the protruding ends of which are usually covered with silver decorations. The Torah is covered with a velvet mantel on which is placed a breastplate, and, not infrequently, a crown of silver.

When the *Sefer Torah* is being read, it is taken out of the ark and carried through the congregation to the *bima*, the elevated stage which usually stands in the centre of the synagogue. The *Sefer Torah* is taken up on to the *bima* and placed on a table, where it is uncovered and read. It is considered an honour to assist at each stage of the taking out of the *Sefer Torah*, and of returning it to the ark; the officials of the synagogue will distribute coveted privileges, as well as the *aliyot*.

In Sephardi communities the *Sefer Torah* is housed in a cylindrical wooden case, richly painted and lacquered. At the time of reading this case is placed upright on the *bima* and opened, allowing the reader to read the exposed vertical columns of text. It is important to note that while Ashkenazi and Sephardi communities have different traditions relating to writing, reading and housing the *Sefer Torah*, the texts of both – comprising 304,805 letters – are identical (with the exception of one letter, which is in dispute).

The *ba'al t'fila*, who leads the service, normally stands in front of the ark (sometimes on the *bima* itself) or to the right of it. It is customary to have an eternal flame (or light) burning within the synagogue. Within the Orthodox tradition men and women pray separately. The separation is sometimes in the form of a dividing screen or partition. In larger synagogues a separate upper balcony for women is often available.

In general, the architecture and internal furnishing of the synagogue reflects many features of the ambient culture. You can find grand, ecclesiastical Gothic façades, with rows of polished pews in Western and Central European communities. In Israel you can see tiny local synagogues with carpet-covered, stone benches duplicating the old places of prayer in Morocco, Iran and Iraq. The expression of Judaism contains a rich diversity, which testifies to its three-and-a-half thousand years of development.

While the synagogue has a level of sanctity, and while it holds a focal point in the life of the religious Jew, a visit to many communities will show that it is all too easy for the building to become a beautiful shell. 'Synagogue' literally means a place of assembly: it is the assembly, rather than the place, which is the essential part of this definition. The presence of God rests upon any assembly of Jews who meet together to study the Torah, or to give praise to Him. The vibrancy and future of Jewish communities is best measured by the level of activity which goes on in the synagogue, not by the splendour of its architecture.

While the architectural detail of the synagogue may vary, reflecting the ambient culture, the basic design – taken from the *mishkan* and the Temples which stood in Jerusalem – can still be clearly recognized. Contemporary Jewish communities are similarly challenged to develop patterns of living which are relevant, inclusive and meaningful, while at the same time retaining the underlying architectural requirement of the Torah and the *mitzvot*. The challenge is substantial, but the growth of relevant, Torah-centred communities in America and Israel indicates that new vistas are possible. Judaism, far from being an ancient religion, is an eternal expression of the love and commitment which exist between God and His special people.

Rabbi Yehoshua ben Levi said: In the future the Holy One will prepare for each righteous person three hundred and ten worlds, as is said [Proverbs 8:21], 'I shall cause those that love Me to inherit substance [the numerical value of this word is 310]; I shall fill their treasure store'. Rabbi Shimon ben Chalafta said: 'The Holy One did not find a stronger way of blessing than through peace, as is written [Psalms 29:1 1], "God gave strength [the Torah] to His people; God blesses His people with peace."'

Okatzim 3:12 (the concluding *Mishna*)

Glossary of Terms Used

In this glossary all defined words are Hebrew unless indicated otherwise. Transliterations have letters with standard English pronunciation, but note that 'ch' is as in the Scottish 'loch' . Plurals indicated in parentheses. Modern Hebrew pronunciation has been used.

Aliya (aliyot)	To go up, either to the reading of the *Torah* or to the land of Israel
Amida	The central prayer which is said while standing
Arba minim	A bundle of four species of plants (citron, palm frond, willow and myrtle twigs) shaken at the festival of *Sukkot*
Ba'al t'filla	Person who leads the congregation in prayer
Ba'al t'shuva	Person who returns to normative Jewish practice
Bar Mitzva	Either a Jewish male who has reached the age of legal majority (13) or the celebration of this event. The equivalent for a young woman (aged 12) is a *Bat Mitzva*

BCE   Before the Common Era, i.e., before the
                       birth of Christ

Bima   Stage on which the *Torah* scroll is read

Baruch Hu   Blessed be the God who is to be blessed: a
                       central part of morning or evening services

Brit mila   Circumcision

CE   Common Era. The time-span which both
                       Jews and Christians share (beginning with
                       the traditional birth of Christ)

Challa (challot)   Literally the portion of dough which was offered
                       in the Temple. Now refers to the braided loaves
                       eaten on the Sabbath or festivals

Chanukka   Eight festivals celebrating the rededication
                       of the Temple after the Maccabee revolt
                       (165 BCE). An increasing number of lights
                       are lit in the window on successive nights
                       of the festival

Chassidim   Literally: 'those who engage in loving-
                       kindness' . A movement stressing a warm,
                       emotional, spiritual approach to Jewish
                       observance founded by the Ba'al Shem Tov
                       (1700–60).

Cholent   (Origin uncertain; the 'ch' is pronounced as in 'chair'.) Hot meat stew eaten on the Sabbath

Chumash   First five books of the Hebrew Bible; the Pentateuch

Chupa   Canopy under which the wedding service is traditionally conducted.

Cohen (cohanim)   Priestly caste who were responsible for Temple services. Since the destruction of the Temple their roles and duties are largely ceremonial

Cohen Ha'gadol   High Priest

Dayan   Qualified rabbinical judge

Davven   (Yiddish) To pray

Gematria   Study of numerical significance in scriptural texts (Hebrew letters have numerical value)

Gerai tzeddek   Sincere and accepted convert to Judaism

Get   Bill of divorce

Golden Medina   (Yiddish) The Golden Land – America

Halacha	Literally 'the walk' ; the way in which Jews are to walk with God – Jewish law
Haftora	Passage from the Prophets read after the Sabbath Torah reading
Hagadda	Traditional text which outlines the events of the Exodus. Read and discussed on the first night(s) of Passover
Havdala	Short service (with wine, sweet smelling spices and braided candles) which marks the end of the Sabbath
Kabbala	Received, mystical exploration of the Torah. Because of its arcane nature it is advised that it should be studied only after 'attaining an age of wisdom'
Kaddish	Aramaic prayer which ends section of public prayer. There are many variations, including one said by mourners
Kashrut	Literally: 'fitness' . Things which are fit for religious use as 'kasher' (or 'kosher')
Kedusha	Response at morning and afternoon prayers expressing the holiness and unity of God
Ketuba	Wedding contract

Ketuvim   Writings of the Prophets

Kiddush   Sanctification of Sabbath or festivals, usually over a cup of wine

Korban (korbanot) Sacrifices in the time of the Temple

Lag b'Omer   Thirty-third day of the Omer; the lively celebration of the death of Rabbi Shimon bar Yochai

Levi   Sect who assisted the *cohanim* in their Temple duties. Today their role is mostly symbolic

Ma'ariv   Evening prayers

Malava malka   (Aramaic) The festive meal which follows the end of the Sabbath

Mashiach   'The anointed one' as in the English 'messiah'

Matza (matzot)   Flour and water kneaded and quickly baked into crisp wafers. Used instead of bread at Passover

Menora   Seven-branched candelabrum of the Temple. The distinctive shape has been incorporated into the seal of the State of Israel

Merkava	Literally 'the chariot'. Mystical speculations based on the vision of Ezekiel, etc.
Mezuza	Handwritten parchment scroll (containing the first two sections of the *Sh'ma*) affixed to most Jewish doorposts
Mincha	Afternoon service
Minhag	Jewish customs hallowed by tradition
Minyan	Minimum of ten adult males required to conduct synagogue services
Mishkan	Portable sanctuary which was used in the desert, following the Exodus
Mishna	First compilation of written law
Musaf	Additional service
Mitzva (mitzvot)	Literally 'commandment' but more meaningfully an opportunity to connect with God

Neshama (neshamot) Soul

Nevi'im	The Prophets
Ni'eela	The concluding service of Yom *Kippur*

Ot	A category of commandments where a physical object ('sign') is given symbolic importance, *e.g. t'fillin*

Parochet	The curtain, usually richly embroidered and adorned, which screens the ark where the *Sefer Torah* is kept

Parsha	A section, usually of the Torah. The weekly section of Torah read on the Sabbath

Pesach	Passover

Purim	Festival celebrating the delivery of the Jews in Persia (see the *Book of Esther*)

Rosh Chodesh	Beginning ('head') of the Jewish month

Rosh Hashana	Beginning ('head') of the Jewish year

Sanhedrin	The supreme court which sat (in Temple times) in Jerusalem

Seder	Order of service on the first night(s) of Passover

Sefer Torah	Scroll containing the first five books of Moses

Simchat Torah   Rejoicing over the law. Ceremony
                     associated with the concluding of the
                     annual Torah reading

Shabbat   The seventh day of creation; the Sabbath
                     which is a Saturday

Shachrit   Morning service

Shatnez   Prohibited mixture of wool and linen fibres.
                     Observant Jews have new clothes checked
                     for this possibility

Shavu'ot   Festival celebrating the giving of the Torah

Sh'chita   The ritual slaughter of animals

Sh'ma Yisrael   'Hear Israel, The Lord is our God: The Lord
                     is one'

Sh'mita   Last year (in a seven-year cycle) when
                     agricultural activity is restricted in Israel

Shiva   Seven-day mourning period

Shofar   Horn made from the horn of a ram

Siddur   Order of prayer; prayer book

Shulchan Aruch	'Prepared table' ; the central, authoritative legal code in Judaism
Sukkot	Festival where Jews try to live in a temporary, thatched dwelling-place
Tallit	Four-cornered prayer shawl worn at morning services
Talmud	Extensive exploration of the *Mishna* in the rabbinical colleges of Babylon. Final, massive work was written (in Aramaic) and edited in the sixth century CE. The central repository of Jewish learning
Talmid chacham	One who is conversant in the arguments of the Talmud; an adept rabbinical scholar
Tanach	Hebrew Bible
Targum	Translation, usually of the *chumash* into Aramaic
T'fillin	Hard leather cubes containing scriptural passages worn at morning prayers (except on the sabbath or festivals)
Tikkun	Repair

Tisha b'Av	Ninth of Av. Day of mourning for the destruction of the Temple
T'shuva	A return to God; repentance
Tzitzit	Knotted woollen cords attached to the corners of certain garments in fulfilment of a Torah injunction
Yahrzeit	(Yiddish) Anniversary of the death of someone
Yom Kippur	The Day of Atonement
Yovel	The fiftieth year in the agricultural cycle. Brought into English as 'jubilee'

Further Reading

This guide is intended to give you a wide coverage of significant aspects of Judaism. If you wish to explore the subject more deeply you might find the following books useful:

Kitov, Rabbi Eliyahu. *The Book of Our Heritage.* (Translated from the Hebrew by Nathan Bulman and Ruth Royde). New York/Jerusalem: Feldheim.

This three-volume work provides a rich, detailed perspective of all aspects of the festivals and fast days.

Hirsch, Rabbi Samson Raphael. *The Pentateuch.* (Translated from the German by Rabbi Isaac Levy). New York: Judaic Press.

This seven-volume work covers the first Five Books of Moses with associated *Haftorot.* Although wordy and a product of the nineteenth century, this work provides a captivating insight into the core text of Judaism. Hirsch writes for a sceptical, non-observant public and stresses symbolic relationships in the text.

Hirsch, Rabbi Samson Raphael. *Horeb.* (Translated from the German by Dayyan Isidor Grunfeld). London: The Soncino Press.

Although first published in 1837, this work still has relevance. It provides a detailed, provocative and extensive classification of the commandments. Dayyan Grunfeld's introduction is particularly helpful.

Kehati, Rabbi Pinchas. *Mishnayot Kehati* (Translated from the Hebrew). New York/Jerusalem: Feldheim.

The most accessible commentary on the *Mishna* which is widely acclaimed by scholars and beginners alike. Although a monumental work, running to more than twenty volumes, individual volumes can be purchased separately.

Hakohen, Yosef Ben Shlomo. *The Universal Jew*. New York: Feldheim.

Through a series of letters a religious son enters into a dialogue with his progressive father. The emphasis is on the concern for the universe which is at the centre of contemporary Jewish thought.

Schwartzbaum, Avraham. *The Bamboo Cradle*. New York/ Jerusalem: Feldheim.

Through the adoption of an abandoned Chinese baby, a young American couple are brought to re-evaluate their Jewish heritage. This sensitive exploration examines many contemporary issues of Jewish life, culture and attitude.

Starr-Glass, David. *Gathered Stones*. New York/Jerusalem: Feldheim.

The autobiographical reflections of a convert to Judaism. It examines the emotional journey as well as the mechanics of the conversion process.

Bauer, Agi. *Black Becomes a Rainbow*. New York/ Jerusalem: Feldheim.

When her daughter accepts a new, Orthodox life-style her mother is confronted with a new set of challenges and fears. This remarkable exploration examines the tensions and potential reconciliation which exist between different generations and traditions within Judaism.

Index